Western Civilization
From Pre-historical Times to the Protestant Reformation

Fr. Peter Samuel Kucer, MSA

En Route Books & Media, LLC
Saint Louis, MO

En Route Books and Media, LLC
5705 Rhodes Avenue
St. Louis, MO 63109

Cover credit: TJ Burdick

Copyright © 2021 Peter Samuel Kucer

Library of Congress Control Number: 2017956388

ISBN-10:0-9994704-3-4
ISBN-13: 978-0-9994704-3-5

All rights reserved.

DEDICATION

In memory of my mother, Roberta Kucer, who instilled in me a love of study and a love of her people, the chosen people.

In addition, I dedicate this book to the members of my community, the Missionaries of the Holy Apostles.

ACKNOWLEDGMENTS

I would particularly like to acknowledge Bishop-Elect Isaac Martinez, MSA, former General of the Missionaries of the Holy Apostles, who gave me permission to publish, and Bishop Christian Rodembourg, MSA, who as the first MSA to be ordained a bishop brought our MSA charism into a deeper ecclesial dimension. Special thanks to Dr. Sebastian Mahfood, OP, president of En Route Books and Media, for publishing this work.

CONTENTS

Chapter 1: Man and Civilization 1

Chapter 2: Jewish Civilization 13

Chapter 3: Jewish Culture 37

Chapter 4: Greek Civilization 55

Chapter 5: Greek Culture 811

Chapter 6: Roman Civilization 113

Chapter 7: Roman Culture 133

Chapter 8: Early Christian Civilization 155

Chapter 9: Fall of Rome and the Rise of Christianity 183

Chapter 10: Medieval World 197

Chapter 11: Renaissance 219

Chapter 12: Fragmentation 247

Index 263

Chapter 1

Man and Civilization

In this chapter, we will focus on two fundamental realities that are foundational to this course, man and civilization.

We will begin with a Catholic concept of what, or more properly, who is man. Then we will take a critical look at the discoveries of paleoanthropology, coming from two Greek words meaning the science of ancient man. In doing this the following prehistoric ages will be introduced: Paleolithic, Neolithic, Bronze Age, and Iron Age.

Since the Iron Age is generally considered the last prehistorical era, before human history was recorded, we will then shift our attention to the study of civilization. The English word civilization is based on the Latin word *civis*. A *civis* was someone who lived in a city, *civitas*.

The study of civilization, therefore, literally means the study of people living in a community, specifically a city. Civilizations that are born around cities rise, decline, and, sometimes, regenerate. A number of theories explain these cycles.

Man

The question of who we are is an essential one to answer when studying Western Civilization from a Catholic perspective. According to official Catholic teaching man is not simply different in degree from other animals. Rather, we are different in kind. In other words, we are not only highly evolved animals. Our ability to reason is not simply due to a slow process of evolution in which consciousness gradually developed. While certain forms of evolutionary theories are not contrary to Church teaching, it is contrary to Church teaching to maintain that the process of evolution, with respect to man, lacked special divine intervention.

As far back as the 1950s, Pope Pius XII in his encyclical letter *Humani Generis* affirmed that evolutionary theory is not contrary to Catholic teaching as long as it is believed that at some point in time God infused a soul into the first man and first woman.

Pope Pius XII in *Humani Generis* explains as follows:

> For these reasons the Teaching Authority of the Church does not forbid that, in conformity with the present state of human sciences and sacred theology, research and discussions, on the part of men experienced in both fields, take place with regard to the doctrine of evolution, in as far as it inquiries into the origin of the

human body as coming from pre-existent and living matter - for the Catholic faith obliges us to hold that souls are immediately created by God. However, this must be done in such a way that the reasons for both opinions, that is, those favorable and those unfavorable to evolution, be weighed and judged with the necessary seriousness, moderation and measure, and provided that all are prepared to submit to the judgment of the Church, to whom Christ has given the mission of interpreting authentically the Sacred Scriptures and of defending the dogmas of faith.[1]

Similarly, Pope Saint John Paul II stated in a General Audience of April 16, 1986, that:

It can therefore be said that, from the viewpoint of the doctrine of the faith, there are no difficulties in explaining the origin of man in regard to the body, by means of the theory of evolution. But it must be added that this hypothesis proposes only a probability, not a scientific certainty. However, the doctrine of faith invariably affirms that man's spiritual soul is created directly by God. According to the hypothesis mentioned, it is possible

---

[1] Pius XII, "Humani Generis," no. 36, August 12, 1950, Vatican, http://w2.vatican.va/content/pius-xii/en/encyclicals/documents/hf_p-xii_enc_12081950_humani-generis.html.

that the human body, following the order impressed by the Creator on the energies of life, could have been gradually prepared in the forms of antecedent living beings. However, the human soul, on which man's humanity definitively depends, cannot emerge from matter, since the soul is of a spiritual nature.[2]

Due to the infusion of the soul, men and women are different in kind from animals who do not have a spiritual soul and, consequently, lack the ability to reason. Human beings also are called to an end that we cannot obtain by our own efforts. More specifically, according to the Catholic faith human beings were created for the end of heaven to be experienced in the beatific vision which we cannot reach without the aid of divine grace. This final cause towards which we are to develop individually and corporately as a civilization profoundly distinguishes us from non-rational animals.

Prehistoric Eras

Prehistory refers to the period prior to written records.

---

[2] John Paul II, "Humans are Spiritual and Corporeal Beings," April 16, 1986, Interdisciplinary Dictionary of Religion and Science, inters.org/printpdf/John-Paul-II-Catechesis-Spiritual-Corporeal.

Chapter 1: Man and Civilization

Note well that the absence of written historical records does not mean that all prehistorical ages were prior to the invention of writing. This is because the presence of a written language does not necessarily mean that those who used this language recorded history. Prehistorical time is typically broken up into three periods: Stone Age, Bronze Age, and Iron Age. The Stone Age is divided into the Old Stone Age, and the New Stone age. During the last two ages, the Bronze and Iron Ages, writing was invented and developed. The dates used for all of these eras are approximate.

Painting of the Stone Age (1882-1885) by Viktor Vasnetsov

During the Old Stone Age (c. 2.5 million years – 10,000 BC) human beings were nomadic. They obtained their food by hunting and gathering hence the name nomadic hunter-gatherers. Archaeologists have acquired evidence that indicates that these nomads used fire, clothing, and tools.

New Stone Age/Neolithic Age

In the Neolithic Age (c. 10,000 – 3,000 BC) some of the nomads settled down and began to farm, raise animals, and grow grain. Weapons for warfare were also made and used during this period. During the last phase of the Neolithic Age, human beings discovered how to use copper for tools. The Copper Age, or Calcolithic age, was replaced by the Bronze Age.

Bronze Age

The main distinctive feature of the Bronze Age (c. 3,000-1000 BC) was smelting of both copper and tin to combine the two metals to create bronze, a metal that is harder than copper. During this age writing was invented, but not necessarily used to record history.

Iron Age

During the Iron Age (c. 1000 – 700 BC) iron was smelted and then shaped into tools or weapons. Agricultural techniques continued to advance in this age.[3]

---

[3] The dates and divisions come from Gavin Lewis, WCIV,

Chapter 1: Man and Civilization 7

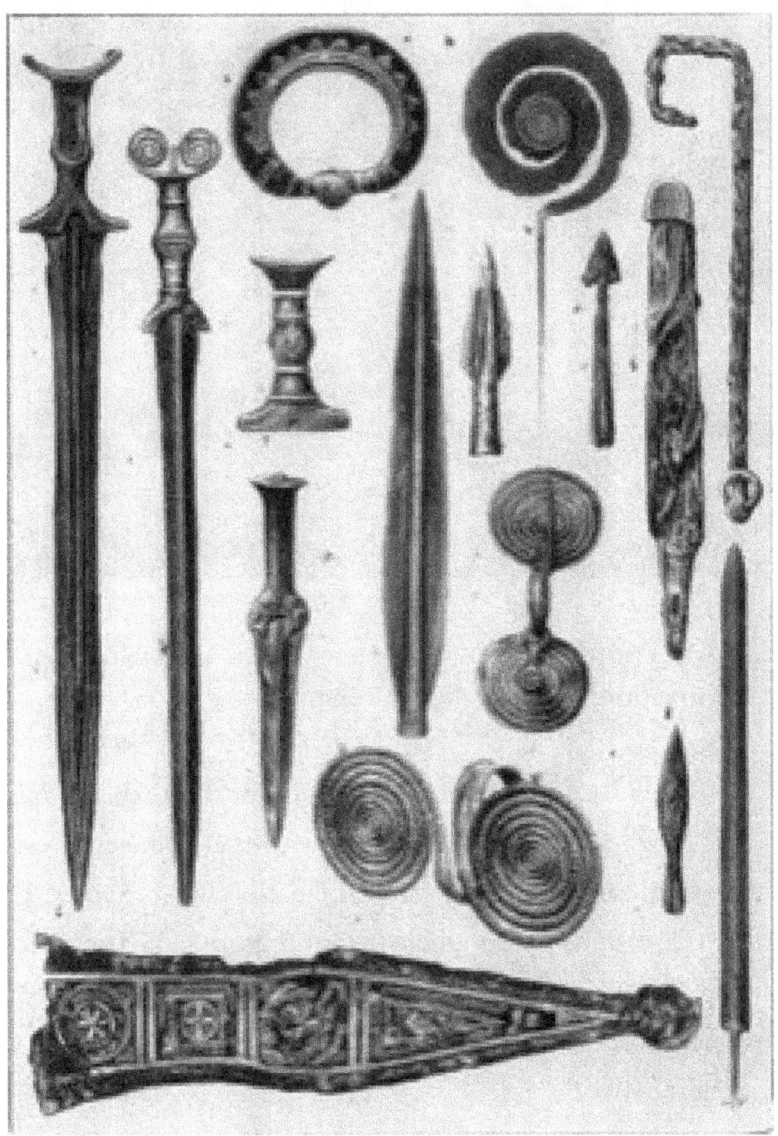

Romanian Bronze Age Ornaments and Weapons

Volume I: To 1700 (Boston: Wadsworth, 2012), 6-7.

Iron Age Coins from England[4]

Civilization: Birth, Decline, Renewal

There are a variety of explanations for the birth, decline, and renewal of the various civilizations that make up Western Civilization. One ancient explanation was proposed by the Greek Stoic philosophers (c. 3rd century BC). The Stoics held that civilizations are fated to undergo historical cycles of birth, decline, death, and rebirth. In the first historical stage, the world emerges out of fire. This is followed by a period of growth according to an inner logic. Eventually, the ordered civilizations that develop out of a chaotic fire are

---

[4] Portable Antiquities Scheme, "A hoard of Iron Age coins from Beverly, East Riding of Yorkshire, England."

Chapter 1: Man and Civilization

once again immersed by flames in order for a new cycle to begin.[5] The German historian Oswald Spengler (1880–1936) modernized the Stoic concept of the history and develop-ment of civilizations by comparing it to a biological organ-ism that has a definite lifespan in which it is born, matures, and inevitably dies.[6]

A very different explanation from both the Stoics and Spengler is linear rather than cyclical. According to a linear understanding of civilizations, often influenced by Hegelian philosophy, while civilizations may rise and fall, the common thread that connects all of them is one of continual progress and improvement as inner conflicts within civilizations are worked out.

The Catholic spiral explanation of history acknowledges both the linear and the cyclical concepts of history and civilizations. According to this more spiral view of history there is direction in history since God created time and destined all of history to be fulfilled in his Son Jesus Christ through the Holy Spirit who "orders all things sweetly" (DRA Wis-

---

[5] "Stoicism," Stanford Encyclopedia of Philosophy, http://plato.stanford.edu/entries/stoicism/; Dirk Baltzly, "Stoicism", The Stanford Encyclopedia of Philosophy (Spring 2014 Edition), Edward N. Zalta (ed.), <http://plato.stanford.edu/archives/spr2014/ entries/stoicism/>.

[6] Oswald Spengler, The Decline of the West, An Abridged Edition, trans. Charles Francis Atkinson (Oxford: Oxford University Press, 1991), 71-72.

dom 8:1) Within this direction are periods of decline that can be due to sin or simply as a result of secondary, natural causes that God permits in his providence to occur. In explaining God's creation, which includes creating out of nothing and sustaining all in existence with God's providence, Bishop Robert Barron writes:

> God's creativity and providence are necessarily expressions of the divine love and hence of the "letting be" of the other. The providential God is not one great cause among many, interfering with the nexus of conditioned causes. We recall the language of the book of Wisdom, how 'sweetly' God exercises his power, operating precisely *through* the realm of secondary causes. If asked, "How do you make a cherry pie," one would say, presumably, "you bring together cherries, sugar, flour, water, fat, and the skill of a baker, and the heat of the oven." Even the religious believer would not say, "You bring together cherries, sugar, flour, God, water, fat, and the skill of the baker, and the heat of the oven." God is not one cause among many, but rather the reason there are cherries, flour, water, fat, the baker, and so on, at all. Hence, it is precisely through those causes and not in competition with them that the providential God works out his purposes.[7]

---

[7] Robert Barron, *Catholicism: A Journey to the Heart of the*

Chapter 1: Man and Civilization

Quiz 1 for Chapter 1

1. Define the word civilization etymologically.

2-3. Explain in at least two ways with reference to one papal document/talk how man is not simply a highly developed animal.

    2.

    3.

4. State the official Catholic teaching on evolution. Include in your answer the soul and consciousness.

4. With reference to writing, define the prehistorical age.

5-7. List the three prehistorical ages and then provide a significant advance for each age.

    5.

Faith (New York: Image Books, 2011), 78.

6.

7.

8-10. Explain and diagram the Stoic, Oswald Spengler's, and the Catholic understanding of the rise and fall of civilizations.

8.

9.

10.

Chapter 2

Jewish Civilization

Introduction

In this chapter and in following chapters, we will study the three principal civilizations that have all significantly contributed to the key characteristics of Western Civilization. We will begin with Jewish civilization before moving on to the Greeks and then to the Romans.

Israelite History

Some scholars claim that the earliest Israelites were polytheists who gave greater honor to a principal God. According to this theory, in time the Israelites gradually developed into monotheists. Other scholars disagree. According to them, the Israelites were monotheists from the earliest days when they became a civilization called together by God Who revealed to them that He is one, as the prophet Isaiah clearly asserts, "I am the Lord, and there is no other; besides me there is no god." (Isaiah 45:5 NRSV) How clear monotheism was in the minds of the earliest Israelites is a subject matter proper to a Sacred Scripture class. For the purpose of this course, it is important to know this topic is debated. In terms of faith, though, even if some or many of the earliest Israelites had pronounced polytheistic tendencies, this would only mean that their beliefs were not in accordance with reality since God is one and there are no other gods despite what people might want to believe. Later, during the time of the New Testament, God as a Trinity of persons in one divine nature was revealed.

Abraham and the Hebrew People

The civilization of God's chosen people was called into existence around 2,000-3,000 BC years ago when a man living in modern day Iraq by the name of Abram was chosen by God.[8] According to a common explanation, during that time the Assyrians, whose central base was situated in modern day Syria, were fighting with the Babylonians, whose center was in Iraq.

---

[8] NRSV Acts 7:2-4. "2 And Stephen replied: 'Brothers[a] and fathers, listen to me. The God of glory appeared to our ancestor Abraham when he was in Mesopotamia, before he lived in Haran, 3 and said to him, 'Leave your country and your relatives and go to the land that I will show you.' 4 Then he left the country of the Chaldeans and settled in Haran. After his father died, God had him move from there to this country in which you are now living."

Chapter 2: Jewish Civilization

While the Assyrians were fighting the Babylonians, a Babylonian man, by the name of Terah (Genesis 11: 26-32; Luke 3:34) was living in the Iraqi City of Ur. (The ruins of this ancient city are still visible.) Fearing for his life, Terah fled (Genesis 11:31) and arrived in the city of Haran, possibly located in modern day Turkey. At the city of Haran, Terah died leaving behind a family and a son by the name of Abram.

Terah's son Abram received a message from God to leave Haran and travel to Canaan, located in modern day Israel (Acts 7:2-4). Abram, soon to be renamed Abraham (Genesis 17:5) to signify an important mission God had given him, travelled to Canaan. He and his family are called Hebrews, possibly in reference to how he arrived in Canaan. To get to Canaan, he had to cross over the Euphrates River.[9] According to one etymological explanation the word Hebrew comes from the root "ʕ-b-r" (עבר) which means "to cross over". This definition is taken to mean that Abraham was called a Hebrew to signify he crossed over a river to reach Canaan.[10]

Abraham's first wife was Sarah. After Sarah did not give birth to a child, she gave her slave Hagar to Abram. The two united and Hagar gave birth to Abram's first born son, Ishmael (Genesis 16: 1-4). Later, Sarah gave birth to Isaac

---

[9] This was done prior to his arrival at Haran.

[10] Rabbi Benjamin Blech, *The Complete Idiot's Guide to Jewish History and Culture* (Indianapolis: Alpha Books, 1999), 23.

(Genesis 21:2). After Sarah died, Abraham married Keturah, with whom he had six additional sons. Notice that the descent of the Israelites does not go through the first born son Ishmael, whom Abraham favored (Genesis 17: 18-21) but through Sarah, the mother of Isaac. Before Isaac was born, God established a covenant with Abraham whose sign is circumcision:

> I will establish my covenant between me and you, and your offspring after you throughout their generations, for an everlasting covenant, to be God to you and to your offspring after you. And I will give to you, and to your offspring after you, the land where you are now an alien, all the land of Canaan, for a perpetual holding; and I will be their God (Genesis 17:7-8 NRSV).

Even though Isaac and not Ishmael was chosen as the first offspring of this covenant, God still blesses Ishmael, "As for Ishmael, I have heard you; I will bless him and make him fruitful and exceedingly numerous; he shall be the father of twelve princes, and I will make him a great nation. But my covenant I will establish with Isaac, whom Sarah shall bear to you at this season next year" (Genesis 17:20-21 NRSV). According to Islam, Muhammad and other Arabs are descendants of Ishmael and his twelve sons.[11] Christians and

---

[11] Rosemary Pennington, "Ishmael and Isaac," December 10,

Chapter 2: Jewish Civilization

Jews, on other hand, trace their Abrahamic spiritual lineage, which may or may not have a physical component, through Isaac.

Jews, Muslims, and Christians all see themselves as descendants of Abraham, just through two different paths.

Jacob and the Israelites

Abraham's second son, Isaac, married Rebekah who gave birth to twins: Esau and Jacob.

Esau was born seconds before Jacob, who emerged clinging onto the heel of his twin brother (Genesis 25:26). Once again, the younger son and not the eldest was chosen by God. Jacob was chosen to be the father of the twelve tribes of Israel. Before this occurs, God changes Jacob's name to Israel after Jacob wrestles with an angel (Genesis 32:28).

Israel had twelve sons, and his daughter, Dinah, from four wives: Leah, Leah's slave Zilpah, Rachel, and Rachel's slave Bilhah. These twelve sons became fathers of the twelve tribes of Israel (Genesis 29:31-49:33). The twelve sons are Reuben, Simeon, Levi, Judah, Dan, Naphtali, Gad, Asher, Issachar, Zebulun, Joseph, and Benjamin. Sometimes, the list of the twelve tribes does not include Levi. As priests, the Levites did not inherit a portion of land and, consequently,

---

2008, Muslim Voices, http://muslimvoices.org/ishmael-islam/, cf. Genesis 25:12-16, 37:25-28.

were to live throughout the lands of all the tribes. In their scattered state, they were to fulfill their priestly role in the service to God and his chosen people. When Levi is not mentioned (Num. 26:4-51), then the two sons of Joseph, Manasseh and Ephraim, are counted as two tribes.

Moses

The twelfth son of Jacob was called Joseph. Due to their father's preferential love for Joseph, his eleven brothers grew increasingly envious of him until they finally sold Joseph as a slave to Ishmaelite merchants traveling to Egypt. In Egypt, Joseph gained the trust of the Pharaoh so much that he was appointed second in command. During a period, predicted by Joseph, when the Middle Eastern lands experienced a drought and crops did not grow, ten of Joseph's brothers were sent by their father to Egypt for food.[12] Without knowing it at first, there they met their brother, Joseph. Even though Joseph recognized his brothers, he graciously received them and provided them with food.

The second time the ten brothers returned they brought with them their youngest brother Benjamin. During this se-

---

[12] For this first trip to Egypt, Benjamin, the youngest, stayed behind.

Chapter 2: Jewish Civilization

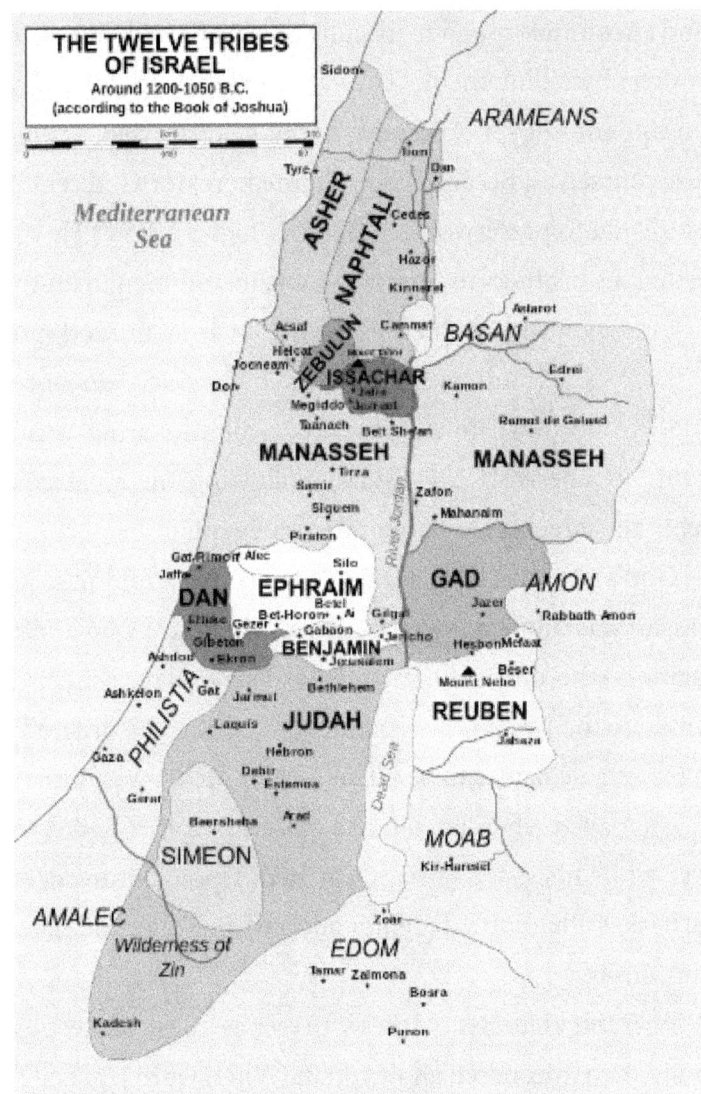

Map of the Twelve Tribes of Israel (c. 1200-1050 BC)[13]

---

[13] "English translation of Hebrew Version. Map of the twelve tribes of Israel, before the move of Dan to the North," map, http://commons.wikimedia.org/wiki/File%3A12_Tribes_of_Israe

cond encounter Joseph mercifully revealed his identity to his brothers by telling them, "I am your brother, Joseph, whom you sold into Egypt. And now do not be distressed, or angry with yourselves, because you sold me here; for God sent me before you to preserve life." (Genesis 45:4-5 NRSV) He then invited his brothers to return to Canaan and then to journey back to Egypt with their entire family. In a vision, God spoke to Jacob/Israel and reassured him by saying, "do not be afraid to go down to Egypt, and I will also bring you up again." (Genesis 46:2-4 NRSV) Following their patriarch, Jacob, the Israelites then migrated to Egypt.

God's promise to Jacob that his people would return to Canaan was fulfilled through Moses. Moses grew up under a Pharaoh who disliked the Israelites and enslaved them. To eliminate the Israelite civilization and culture, he ordered all Israelite male babies to be killed. When Moses was born, his life was saved when his mother placed him in a basket in a river while his sister Miriam watched. Upon coming across the basket, Pharaoh's daughter adopted the baby and named him Moses.

Pharaoh tolerated Moses's presence until Moses, as a young man, murdered an Egyptian. When word reached the Pharaoh of Moses's deed, he ordered Moses to be found and killed. Moses fled for his life and sought refuge with the Midianites where he married a Midianite woman named

---

l_Map.svg

Chapter 2: Jewish Civilization

Zipporah. While Moses was working as a shepherd on Mount Horeb, God revealed Himself to him in a burning bush whose flames lit it up but did not consume it. After Moses removed his sandals, as a sign of respect, God said:

> I have observed the misery of my people who are in Egypt; I have heard their cry on account of their taskmasters. Indeed, I know their sufferings, and I have come down to deliver them from the Egyptians, and to bring them up out of that land to a good and broad land, a land flowing with milk and honey, to the country of the Canaanites... (Exodus 3: 7-8 NRSV).

Despite protesting that he had a speech impediment,[14] Moses, aided by his brother Aaron, known for his eloquence, led the Israelites out of Egypt through the Sinai desert for forty years to the Jordan River. The Israelite exodus out of Egypt to the promised land of Canaan took place sometime during the Egyptian New Empire era (1500-1000 BC) consisting of the eleventh to seventeenth dynasties (XI-XVII).[15] At Mount Sinai, God revealed to Moses the written

---

[14] Genesis 4:10 "But Moses said to the Lord, 'O my Lord, I have never been eloquent, neither in the past nor even now that you have spoken to your servant; but I am slow of speech and slow of tongue.'"

[15] *The Navarre Bible: The Pentateuch* (Princeton: Scepter

Torah, the core of which is the Ten Commandments (Exodus 20:1-17; Deuteronomy 5:4-21) and, according to Jewish tradition, the oral Torah.

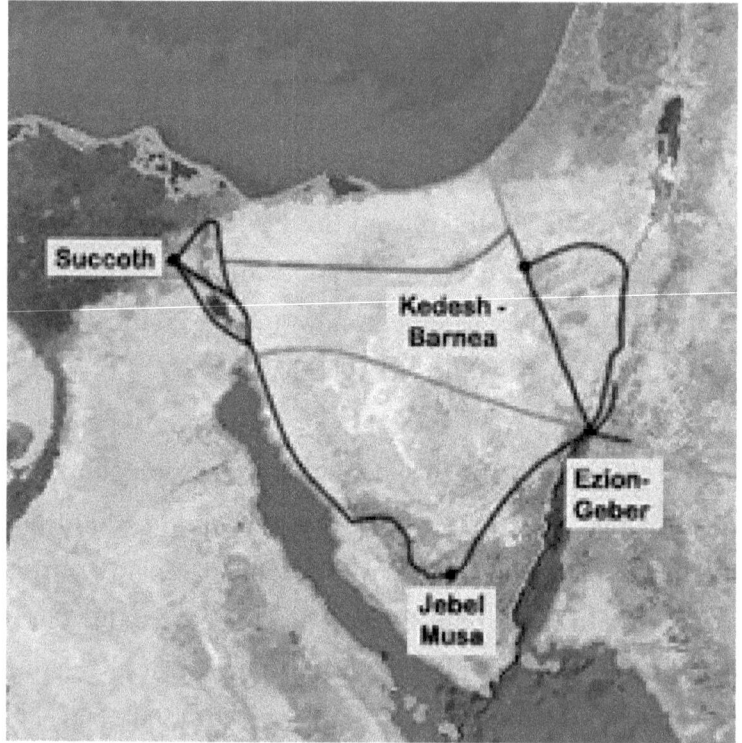

Possible Routes of the Exodus[16]

Publishers, 1999), 238-239.

[16] Map generated by ThaThinker, http://commons.wikimedia.org/wiki/File:Exodus_Map.jpg

Chapter 2: Jewish Civilization 23

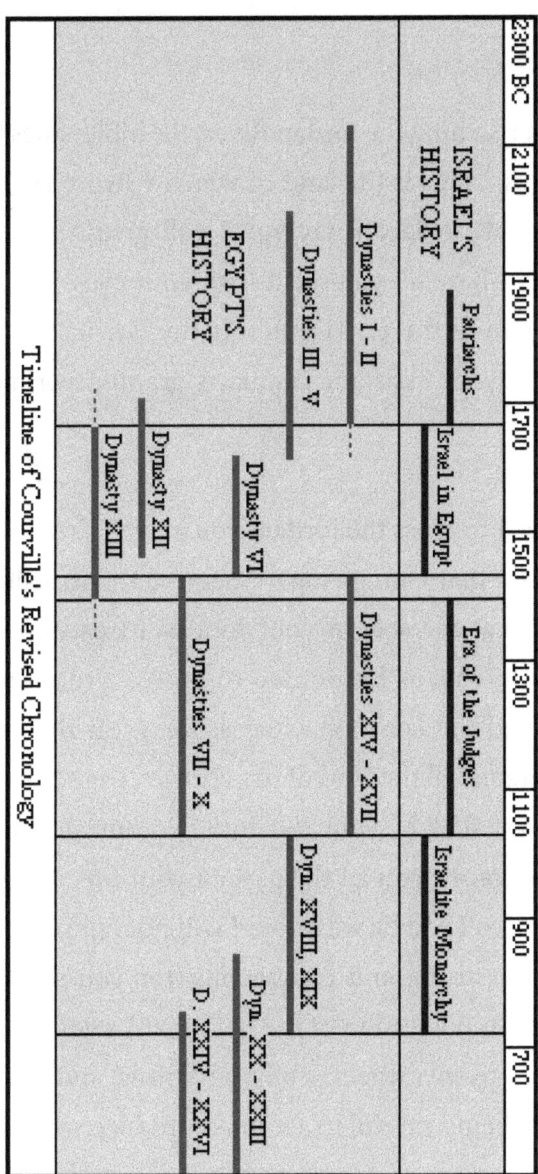

Approximate Timeline of Israelite History[17]

---

[17] Tuckerresearch, "Courville.gif," timeline, http://commons.wikimedia.org/wiki/File%3ACourville.gif

Joshua

Upon reaching the Jordan River, the bible states that God told Moses, "This is the land of which I swore to Abraham, to Isaac, and to Jacob, saying, 'I will give it to your descendants'; I have let you see it with your eyes, but you shall not cross over there." (Deuteronomy 34: 4 NRSV) Once Moses died, his assistant Joshua is granted permission by God to:

> proceed to cross the Jordan, you and all this people, into the land that I am giving to them, to the Israelites. Every place that the sole of your foot will tread upon I have given to you, as I promised to Moses. From the wilderness and the Lebanon as far as the great river, the river Euphrates, all the land of the Hittites, to the Great Sea in the west shall be your territory. No one shall be able to stand against you all the days of your life. As I was with Moses, so I will be with you; I will not fail you or forsake you. Be strong and courageous; for you shall put this people in possession of the land that I swore to their ancestors to give them. Only be strong and very courageous, being careful to act in accordance with all the law that my servant Moses commanded you; do not turn from it to the right hand or to the left, so that you may be successful wherever you go. This book of the law shall not depart out of your mouth; you shall meditate on it

day and night, so that you may be careful to act in accordance with all that is written in it. (Joshua 1: 2-8 NRSV)

From a Catholic perspective, the name of Joshua is of great importance since the English name Jesus originally, via Latin and Greek, comes from the Hebrew name Joshua (*Yehoshua*), meaning God saves.[18] The names Joshua and Jesus, therefore, are interchangeable with one another. According to the Catholic faith, Jesus Christ as the new Joshua fulfills the Joshua of old by not leading his people over a body of water into an earthly promised land but instead by leading His people over the waters of death into the promised land of heaven.

Judges

The Book of Joshua is followed by the Book of Judges, named after twelve leaders of Israel. These leaders were not kings with a centralized government but rather highly gifted individuals that God inspired to direct His people when needed. The six judges that are written about in detail are Othniel, Ehud, Deborah (who was helped by Barak), Gideon, Jephthah, and Samson. Along with these six "major judges,"

---

[18] "Jesus," Online Etymology Dictionary, Interlinear NIV Hebrew-English Old Testament (Numbers 14:30). http://etymonline.com/index.php,

six other minor judges are mentioned in passing. In 1 Samuel, the last two judges are described, Eli and Samuel, who is also considered a prophet.

Near the end of Samuel's life, the Israelites repeatedly demanded that, "There must be a king over us. We too must be like other nations, with a king to rule us and to lead us in warfare and fight our battles" (1 Samuel 8: 19-20). God indicated his displeasure with this request by telling Samuel, "It is not you they reject [as Judge and prophet], they are rejecting me as their king" (1 Samuel 8: 7). The Lord then added, "Now grant their request; but at the same time, warn them solemnly and inform them of the rights of the king who will rule them" (1 Samuel 8: 9). The first king whom God directed Samuel to anoint was Saul, from the tribe of Benjamin.

Major Judges	**Minor Judges**	**Last Two Judges**
Othniel	Shamgar	Eli
Ehud	Tola	Samuel
Deborah	Jair	
Gideon	Ibzan	
Jephtah	Elon	
Samson	Abdon	

Chapter 2: Jewish Civilization

Kings

As the chart below indicates, the Israelites only remained united as a people under the first three kings who lived around the turn of the century (1000 BC): Saul, David, and Solomon. After Solomon died, his united kingdom was divided into two. Jeroboam I ruled over the northern lands, called Israel, whose capital city was Samaria. Rehoboam, Solomon's son, ruled over the southern lands, called Judah, whose capital city was Jerusalem.

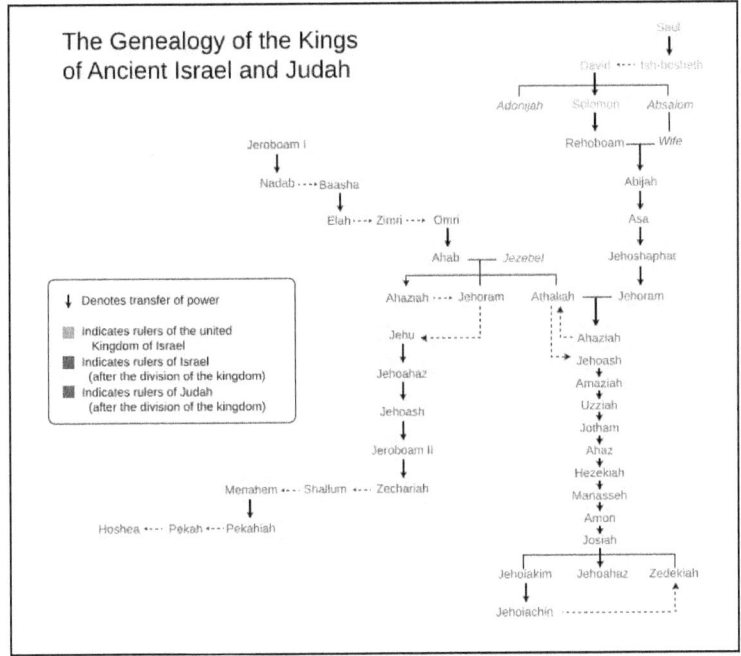

The genealogy of the kings of Israel and Judah.
Based on a literal interpretation of 1 and 2 Kings.[19]

---

[19] http://commons.wikimedia.org/wiki/File%3AGenealogy_

Assyrian Exile

In 722 BC, the Assyrian King Sargon II defeated the Northern Kingdom of Israel and deported its people. The map below shows the location of the Assyrian Empire, north of Israel.

Map showing the Kingdoms of Israel (north) and Judah (south), ancient Southern Levant borders and ancient cities such as Urmomium and Jerash. The map shows the region in the 9th century BCE.[20]

---

of_the_kings_of_Israel_and_Judah.svg

[20] http://commons.wikimedia.org/wiki/File%3AKingdoms_of_Israel_and_Judah_map_830.svg

Babylonian Captivity and the Jewish People

A few centuries later, the Southern Kingdom of Judah also was exiled by the Babylonians (c. 598-586 BC). To make matters worse, in c. 586 BC, to the great horror of the Jewish people, the Babylonian King Nebuchadnezzar destroyed Jerusalem. Notice that the term Jewish people is used here, and not Israel. This is because the tribes that consisted of the Northern Kingdom of Israel are considered lost to history (Reuben, Issachar, Zebulun, Dan, Naphtali, Gad, Asher, Ephraim, Manasseh, and some people from the landless, priestly tribe of Levi).

The remaining two tribes of Judah and Benjamin (plus members from the landless, priestly tribe of Levi) belonged to the Southern Kingdom of Judah. Only people of the Southern Kingdom of Judah were able to keep their identity intact as a civilization. At least this is what is commonly stated. The people of Samaria who claim to be descendants of the Northern Tribe of Israel think otherwise.

The Persians and Cyrus the Great

The survival of the Jewish people as a civilization was providentially helped when in 538 BC the Persian King Cyrus II (reigned 559-530 BC) defeated the Babylonian Empire and permitted the Jews to return to their homeland. The Edict of Cyrus, which officially gave permission to the Jews to return, is described in the bible as divinely inspired (Ezra 1:1-4). By 516 BC, the building of the Second Temple was complete. In 458 BC, Ezra the priest was allowed by the Persian King Artaxerxes I (reigned 465-424 BC) to lead more Jews back to Jerusalem. He was followed, in 445, by Nehemiah who, acting as the ruler of Jerusalem, oversaw the rebuilding of its walls.[21]

Northern Kingdom of Israel (ends in 722 BC)	Southern Kingdom of Judah (ends in 586 BC)	Tribe Shared by Both Kingdoms
1. Reuben	1. Judah	1. Levi
2. Issachar	2. Benjamin	
3. Zebulun		
4. Dan		
5. Naphtali		
6. Gad		
7. Asher		
8. Ephraim (Joseph's son)		
9. Manasseh (Joseph's son)		

---

[21] H.H. Ben-Sasson, *A History of the Jewish People* (Cambridge: Harvard University Press, 1976), 166, 172-176.

Greek Rule, Hasmonean State, Roman Rule

In the following century, the Persian Empire was replaced by a Greek Empire when the Northern Macedonian Alexander the Great (356-323 BC) defeated the Persians. As emperor, Alexander continued the Persian policy of religious toleration. He even recognized the Jewish high priest of Jerusalem as the Jewish representative to his rule.[22] His emperorship, though, was short-lived, and in 323 BC, he died. He was only 32 years old. After his death, his empire became divided into four regions ruled by Cassander, Lysimachus, Ptolemy, and Seleucus I Nicator. Out of these four regions emerged two dominant empires: the northeastern, Syrian Seleucid Empire, and the southwestern, Egyptian Ptolemy Empire.[23]

The Jewish people living in the province of Judea, first established by the Persians,[24] were sandwiched in between these two Greek empires in competition with one another. Since the Ptolemaic empire adhered more to the Persian's and Alexander the Great's policy of religious tolerance, many Jews migrated westward to the Egyptian land and settled around the Egyptian city of Alexandria, named in

---

[22] Ben-Sasson, *A History of the Jewish People*, 181.

[23] Philip Freeman, *Alexander the Great* (New York: Simon & Schuster, 2011), 321-323, 340.

[24] Ben-Sasson, *A History of the Jewish People*, 191.

honor of Alexander the Great.

When the Seleucid Emperor Antiochus Epiphanes (reigned 175-164) took power, he sought ways to control the Judean state that was between his empire and the Ptolemaic Empire. One way he did this was by replacing Judea's high priest, Onias III, with the more malleable Jason, brother of Onias III. Jason set out to change Jerusalem into a Greek city, complete with a Greek gymnasium, and even renamed it Antiochia, in honor of Antiochus. 2 Maccabees describes other ways in which Jason tried to cause the Jewish people to leave behind their Judaism and embrace Greek culture and religion.

> He set aside the existing royal concessions to the Jews, secured through John the father of Eupolemus, who went on the mission to establish friendship and alliance with the Romans; and he destroyed the lawful ways of living and introduced new customs contrary to the law. He took delight in establishing a gymnasium right under the citadel, and he induced the noblest of the young men to wear the Greek hat. There was such an extreme of Hellenization and increase in the adoption of foreign ways because of the surpassing wickedness of Jason, who was ungodly and no true high priest, that the priests were no longer intent upon their service at the altar. Despising the sanctuary and neglecting the sacrifices, they hurried to take part in the unlawful proceedings in the wrestling

arena after the signal for the discus-throwing, disdaining the honors prized by their ancestors and putting the highest value upon Greek forms of prestige. For this reason heavy disaster overtook them, and those whose ways of living they admired and wished to imitate completely became their enemies and punished them. It is no light thing to show irreverence to the divine laws—a fact that later events will make clear. (2 Maccabees 4:11-17 NRSV)

Desiring to speed up the assimilation of the Jewish people to Greek ways, in 167 BC Emperor Antiochus banned the practice of Judaism. Those found guilty of circumcising boys and/or observing the Jewish Sabbath were, he ordered, to be killed. He also forced Jews to participate in pagan rites and to eat pork. Finally, he had the Jerusalem Temple desecrated and consecrated to the Greek God Zeus.[25]

The Jewish priest Mattathias responded by rebelling against Antiochus's dictatorship. In 165 BC, when Mattathias died, his defiance was continued by his son Judas Maccabee, who wisely became an ally of the Romans who were rapidly rising in power. In 161 BC, the Romans, who had conquered Macedonia a few years prior in 168 BC, agreed to be an ally. Aided by the Romans, in 140 BC the Jewish people regained their lands and established the Hasmonean dynasty that

---

[25] Ben-Sasson, *A History of the Jewish People*, 204.

lasted up until 37 BC when the Romans installed King Herod the Great as King of Judea (reigned 37-4 BC).[26]

Quiz 2 for Chapter 2

1-10. Trace the history of the Hebrew people up until the time they are properly called Israelites. Include in your explanation the following: Iraq, Abram, Canaan, Abraham, Sarah, Hagar, circumcision, Arabs, Jews, and Christians.

11-23. Trace the history of the Israelites from Jacob up to the Babylonian Exile. Include the following: Isaac, Jacob, twelve sons of Jacob, Joseph, Egypt, Moses, Joshua, Canaan, Judges, Kings, United Kingdom, Divided Kingdom, and Assyrian Exile.

---

[26] Ben-Sasson, *A History of the Jewish People*, 185-200, 212, 216; David Flusser, and R. Steven Notley, *The Sage from Galilee: Rediscovering Jesus' Genius* (Grand Rapids: Wm. B. Eerdmans Publishing Co., 2007), 166-167.

Chapter 2: Jewish Civilization

24-26. Identify the following:

24.	25.	26.
1. Reuben	1. Judah	1. Levi
2. Issachar	2. Benjamin	
3. Zebulun		
4. Dan		
5. Naphtali		
6. Gad		
7. Asher		
8. Ephraim (Joseph's son)		
9. Manasseh (Joseph's son)		

27. In relationship to the Jewish people, who was Cyrus the Great, and what did the edict he issued concerning the Jewish people allow?

28. What empire in the 300s BC defeated and replaced the Persian Empire?

29. What empire in the 100s BC defeated and replaced the Greek Empire?

Chapter 3

Jewish Culture

Introduction

Various aspects of Jewish culture have made a deep impact on Western Civilization. The following are some of the most important contributions that Judaism has made to Western Civilization: belief in one Creator, Sacred Scriptures, reverence of the human being, reverence for law (oral and written), system of justice, and care for the poor. All six of these contributions are expressed in the Jewish belief called *Tikkun Olam* which means healing the world by making it a better place.[27]

---

[27] The Institute of Curriculum Services, a US Jewish service for "accurate Jewish content in schools" lists and explains the following five ways in which Western Civilization has been positively affected by Jewish culture. Individual worth, rule of law, fair trail, charity, and healing the world. "Judaism and Western Civilization," Institute of Curriculum Services, http://www.icsresources.org/content/curricula/JudaismAndWesternCivilization.pdf.

One Creating God who Loves Creation

The inspired author of Genesis wrote the first verse with "In the beginning God created the heavens and the earth." (Genesis 1:1 NASB) Then, the inspired author proceeds to correct rival epics, such as the *Enuma Elish*. Errors contained in these epics on the beginning of the universe include that there are many Gods, human beings are not loved by the Gods, human beings are manipulated by Gods, matter is evil, and there is a Sun God and a moon God etc.

God inspired the Genesis writer to correct the errors listed above by teaching that there is only one God. God loves his creation. God especially loves men and women who are "very good" (Genesis 1:31 NASB). The Sun and all physical things are not Gods but only created by God, and matter is not evil.[28]

Comparing and contrasting the Genesis account of creation, Joshua J. Mark writes of the *Enuma Elish's* Mesopotamian Gods:

---

[28] Robert Spitzer, "Teaching Science and Faith – Conflict or Confluence? For High School Science and Religion Teachers," Institute for Theological Encounter with Science and Technology and the Magis Center, http://mp125118.cdn.mediaplatform.com/125118/wc/mp/4000/5592/5599/45578/Archive/default.htm.

Chapter 3: Jewish Culture

In ancient Mesopotamia, the meaning of life was for one to live in concert with the gods. Humans were created as co-laborers with their gods to hold off the forces of chaos and to keep the community running smoothly. According to the Mesopotamian creation myth, the Enuma Elish, (meaning, 'When on High') life began after an epic struggle between the elder gods and the younger. In the beginning there was only water swirling in chaos and undifferentiated between fresh and bitter. These waters separated into two distinct principals: the male principal, Apsu, which was fresh water and the female principal, Tiamat, salt water. From the union of these two principals all the other gods came into being.

These younger gods were so loud in their daily concourse with each other that they came to annoy the elders, especially Apsu and, on the advice of his Vizier, he decided to kill them. Tiamat, however, was shocked at Apsu's plot and warned one of her sons, Ea, the god of wisdom and intelligence. With the help of his brothers and sisters, Ea put Apsu to sleep and then killed him. Out of the corpse of Apsu, Ea created the earth and built his home (though, in later myths 'the Apsu' came to mean the watery home of the gods or the realm of the gods). Tiamat, upset now over Apsu's death, raised the forces of chaos to destroy her children herself. Ea and his siblings fought against Tiamat and her allies, her champion,

Quingu, the forces of chaos and Tiamat's creatures, without success until, from among them, rose the great storm god Marduk. Marduk swore he would defeat Tiamat if the gods would proclaim him their king. This agreed to, he entered into battle with Tiamat, killed her and, from her body, created the sky. He then continued on with the act of creation to make human beings from the remains of Quingu as help-mates to the gods.[29]

Sacred Scriptures

The Jewish bible, or Hebrew Scriptures, form most of what Christianity considers as the Old Testament. The following charts compare and contrast the Jewish bible with the Christian Old Testament: Protestant, Orthodox, and Catholic.[30]

---

[29] Joshua J. Mark, "Mesopotamian Religion," *Ancient History Encyclopedia.* http://www.ancient.eu/Mesopotamian_Religion/

[30] Data for the charts but not the charts themselves comes from the following site. Felix Just, "Jewish and Christian Bibles: A Comparative Chart," *Catholic Resources for Bible, Liturgy, Art, and Theology,* http://catholic- resources.org/Bible/Heb-Xn-Bibles.htm.

Chapter 3: Jewish Culture

	Jewish
Name for all books	**TaNak** or Tanakh (Acronym for Torah Nevi'im and Khetuvim or Law/Teaching, Prophets, and Writings)
Name for the first Five Books	**Torah**
Book 1	Bereshit
Book 2	Shemot
Book 3	VayYikra
Book 4	BaMidbar
Book 5	Davarim
Former Prophets	**Nevi'im**
Book 6	Joshua
Book 7	Judges
Book 8	Samuel (1&2)
Book 9	Kings (1&2)
Latter Prophets	**Nevi'im**
Book 10	Isaiah
Book 11	Jeremiah
Book 12	Ezekiel
Book 13	The Book of the Twelve: Hosea, Joel, Amos, Obadiah, Jonah, Micah, Nahum, Habakkuk, Zephaniah, Haggai, Zechariah, Malachi
Writings	**Khetuvim**
Book 14	Psalms (150)
Book 15	Proverbs
Book 16	Job
Book 17	Song of Solomon

Book 18	Ruth
Book 19	Lamentations
Book 20	Ecclesiastes
Book 21	Esther
Book 22	Daniel (12 chapters)
Book 23	Ezra-Nehemiah
Book 24	Chronicles (1&2)

	Protestant Bible		Orthodox Bible		Catholic Bible
Name for the first 5 Books	Pentateuch (from Greek meaning five books)		Pentateuch		Pentateuch
Bk 1	Genesis	Bk 1	Genesis	Bk 1	Genesis
Bk 2	Exodus	Bk 2	Exodus	Bk 2	Exodus
Bk 3	Leviticus	Bk 3	Leviticus	Bk 3	Leviticus
Bk 4	Numbers	Bk 4	Numbers	Bk 4	Numbers
Bk 5	Deuteronomy	Bk 5	Deuteronomy	Bk 5	Deuteronomy
Historical Books					
Bk 6	Joshua	Bk 6	Joshua	Bk 6	Joshua
Bk 7	Judges	Bk 7	Judges	Bk 7	Judges
Bk 8	Ruth	Bk 8	Ruth	Bk 8	Ruth
Bk 9	1 Samuel	Bk 9	1 Kingdoms	Bk 9	1 Samuel
Bk 10	2 Samuel	Bk 10	2 Kingdoms	Bk 10	2 Samuel
Bk 11	1 Kings	Bk 11	3 Kingdoms	Bk 11	1 Kings
Bk 12	2 Kings	Bk 12	4 Kingdoms	Bk 12	2 Kings

Bk 13	1 Chronicles	Bk 13	1 Chronicles	Bk 13	1 Chronicles
Bk 14	2 Chronicles	Bk 14	2 Chronicles	Bk 14	2 Chronicles
Bk 15	Ezra	Bk 15	1 Esdras	Bk 15	Ezra
Bk 16	Nehemiah	Bk 16	2 Esdras (Erza + Nehemiah)	Bk 16	Nehemiah
Bk 17	Esther (Short Version)	Bk 17	Esther (Long Version)	Bk 17	Esther (Long Version)
		Bk 18	Judith	Bk 18	Tobit
		Bk 19	Tobit	Bk 19	Judith
		Bk 20	1 Maccabees	Bk 20	1 Maccabees
		Bk 21	2 Maccabees	Bk 21	2 Maccabees
		Bk 22	3 Maccabees		
		Bk 23	4 Maccabees		

Name of Wisdom Literature	**Wisdom Books**	Name of Wisdom Lit	**Poetic Books**	Name of Wisdom Lit	**Wisdom Books**
Bk 18	Job	Bk 24	Psalms (151)	Bk 22	Job
Bk 19	Psalms (150)	Bk 25	Odes (w/ Prayer of Manasseh)	Bk 23	Psalms (150)
Bk 20	Proverbs	Bk 26	Proverbs	Bk 24	Proverbs
Bk 21	Ecclesiastes	Bk 27	Ecclesiastes	Bk 25	Ecclesiastes
Bk 22	Song of Solomon	Bk 28	Song of Solomon	Bk 26	Song of Solomon
		Bk 29	Job	Bk 27	Wisdom of Solomon

				Bk 30	Wisdom of Solomon	Bk 28	Sirach (Ecclesiasticus)
				Bk 31	Sirach (Ecclesiasticus)	Bk 29	Isaiah
				Bk 32	Psalms of Solomon	Bk 30	Jeremiah
Prophets						Bk 31	Lamentations
Bk 23	Isaiah	Bk 33	Hosea			Bk 32	Baruch (with Letter of Jeremiah)
Bk 24	Jeremiah	Bk 34	Amos			Bk 33	Ezekiel
Bk 25	Lamentations	Bk 35	Micah			Bk 34	Daniel (14 chapters)
Bk 26	Ezekiel	Bk 36	Joel			Bk 35	Hosea
Bk 27	Daniel (12 chapters)	Bk 37	Obadiah			Bk 36	Joel
Bk 28	Hosea	Bk 38	Jonah			Bk 37	Amos
Bk 29	Joel	Bk 39	Nahum			Bk 38	Obadiah
Bk 30	Amos	Bk 40	Habakkuk			Bk 39	Jonah
Bk 31	Obadiah	Bk 41	Zephaniah			Bk 40	Micah
Bk 32	Jonah	Bk 42	Haggai			Bk 41	Nahum
Bk 33	Micah	Bk 43	Zechariah			Bk 42	Habakkuk
Bk 34	Nahum	Bk 44	Malachi			Bk 43	Zephaniah
Bk 35	Habakkuk	Bk 45	Isaiah			Bk 44	Haggai

Bk 36	Zephaniah	Bk 46	Jeremiah	Bk 45	Zechariah
Bk 37	Haggai	Bk 47	Baruch	Bk 46	Malachi
Bk 38	Zechariah	Bk 48	Lamentations	Bk 47	
Bk 39	Malachi	Bk 49	Letter of Jeremiah	Bk 48	
		Bk 50	Ezekiel	Bk 49	
		Bk 51	Daniel	Bk 50	
		Bk 52	Susanna	Bk 51	
		Bk 53	Bel and the Dragon		

The Hebrew Scriptures and the Old Testament, which are not exactly equal as evident above, have been interpreted in a variety of ways throughout the history of Western Civilization. The three most common are as follows: not-inspired, dictation theory, and participation theory.

- o Those who view the bible as simply a book like any other do not believe it is divinely inspired and therefore hold that it does not contain any divine revelation.
- o The opposite of this skeptical view is the dictation theory. According to the dictation theory, God inspired every single word the authors of scripture wrote. Sometimes, this leads people to assert that the bible teaches not only salvific truth but also scientific truth in a precise manner as we currently define

science.
- According to the participation theory of biblical inspiration, human intellects with their historical categories and understanding of the world participated in writing the divinely inspired text. In collaborating with man, God inspired the human author but did not give words to the author. He respected the author's categories and words. With divine condescension God allowed the human authors to use historically conditioned categories and words when writing down the sacred inspired truths. This manner of reception follows the well-known principle of St. Thomas Aquinas, that "whatever is received is received in the mode of the receiver." As clearly stated in Pope Pius XII's *Divino Afflante Spiritu,* God inspired the authors to teach sacred truths necessary for salvation. Because of His respect for the human author's mental categories and language, God did not inspire the biblical authors to accurately describe the physical universe in a precise, modern scientific manner. Rather, He accommodated his truths according to human historically conditioned concepts so that we can understand Him.[31]

---

[31] Robert Spitzer, "Teaching Science and Faith – Conflict or Confluence? For High School Science and Religion Teachers," Institute for Theological Encounter with Science and Techno-

Chapter 3: Jewish Culture

~ Divino Afflante Spiritu #43 ~

The first and greatest care of Leo XIII was to set forth the teaching on the truth of the Sacred Books and to defend it from attack. Hence with grave words did he proclaim that there is no error whatsoever if the sacred writer, speaking of things of the physical order "went by what sensibly appeared" as the Angelic Doctor says, speaking either "in figurative language, or in terms which were commonly used at the time, and which in many instances are in daily use at this day, even among the most eminent men of science." For "the sacred writers, or to speak more accurately - the words are St. Augustine's - the Holy Spirit, Who spoke by them, did not intend to teach men these things - that is the essential nature of the things of the universe things in no way profitable to salvation"; which principle "will apply to cognate sciences, and especially to history," that is, by refuting, "in a somewhat similar way the fallacies of the adversaries and defending the historical truth of Sacred Scripture from their attacks." Nor is the sacred writer to be taxed with error, if "copyists have made mistakes in the text of the Bible," or, "if the real meaning of a passage remains ambiguous."

---

logy & the Magis Center, http://mp125118.cdn.Mediaplatform.com/125118/wc/mp/4000/5592/5599/45578/Archive/default.htm.

Finally, it is absolutely wrong and forbidden "either to narrow inspiration to certain passages of Holy Scripture, or to admit that the sacred writer has erred," since divine inspiration "not only is essentially incompatible with error but excludes and rejects it as absolutely and necessarily as it is impossible that God Himself, the supreme Truth, can utter that which is not true. This is the ancient and constant faith of the Church."[32]

Reverence of the Human Being

Ancient Assyrian, Babylonian, Persian, Indian, Greek, Roman, and many other civilizations assumed that an individual's worth is based on their status in society. In some civilizations, an elaborate caste system determines what a person's value is.

Other cultures are less explicit but nonetheless have their own caste like way of determining a person's value. As we will see in a subsequent chapter, in the century before the birth of Christ, the Roman Stoic Cicero argued that everyone has, by natural law, equal value. Way before this assertion of reason, the Jewish people received revelation from God that

---

[32] Pope Pius XII, "Divino Afflante Spiritu," 1943, no. 3, Vatican, http://w2.vatican.va/content/pius- xii/en/encyclicals/documents/hf_p-xii_enc_30091943_divino-afflante-spiritu.html

all human beings are of equal value since they are made in the image and likeness of God as Genesis 1:26-27 affirms:

> Then God said, "Let us make humankind in our image, according to our likeness; and let them have dominion over the fish of the sea, and over the birds of the air, and over the cattle, and over all the wild animals of the earth, and over every creeping thing that creeps upon the earth." So God created humankind in his image, in the image of God he created them; male and female he created them. (NRSV)

Reverence for Law, System of Justice, and Care for the Poor

The Western concept of a rule of law that equally applies to all is also in part due to the Jewish civilization's value of law. It is also, as will be seen later, due to the Roman value of law and order. Unlike the Roman appreciation of law to keep order in their empire by reducing the likelihood of rebellion from people who deem themselves not being treated fairly, the Jewish recognition of law's importance stems not from practical concerns but, according to Sacred Scripture and Jewish oral tradition, out of reverence for God.

The Jewish laws were reflected in a system of justice, complete with a court system, by which individuals accused of crimes had assurance they would be treated fairly. The importance in the West of a fair trial is partly due to this aspect of Jewish life.[33] Below are but a few of the Court and Judicial *mitzvot* (Hebrew for laws) from the traditionally determined 613 *Mitzvot* that come from the Torah (first five books of the bible).

~ Jewish Legal System ~

1. "You must not be partial in judging: hear out the small and the great alike; you shall not be intimidated by anyone, for the judgment is God's. Any case that is too hard for you, bring to me, and I will hear it." (Deuteronomy 1:17 NRSV)
2. "You shall appoint judges and officials throughout your tribes, in all your towns that the LORD your God is giving you, and they shall render just decisions for the people." (Deuteronomy 16:18 NRSV)
3. "You must carry out fully the law that they (Jewish High Court) interpret for you or the ruling that they announce to you; do not turn aside from the decision that they announce to you, either to the right or to the left." (Deuteronomy 17:11 NRSV)
4. "A single witness shall not suffice to convict a person of any crime or wrongdoing in connection with any offense that may be committed. Only on the evidence

---

[33] The Institute of Curriculum Services.

of two or three witnesses shall a charge be sustained." (Deuteronomy 19:15 NRSV)

5. "You shall not render an unjust judgment; you shall not be partial to the poor or defer to the great: with justice you shall judge your neighbor." (Leviticus 19:15 NRSV)

6. "You shall not deprive a resident alien or an orphan of justice; you shall not take a widow's garment in pledge. Remember that you were a slave in Egypt and the Lord your God redeemed you from there; therefore I command you to do this." (Deuteronomy 24:17-18 NRSV).[34]

Jewish law also required that the poor and vulnerable be not harmed, be provided with means to help themselves, and be given aid when needed. Below are a few of the pertinent *mitzvot* from the Torah.

1. "You shall not wrong or oppress a resident alien, for you were aliens in the land of Egypt. You shall not abuse any widow or orphan." (Exodus 22:21-22 NRSV)

2. "When you reap the harvest of your land, you shall

---

[34] For a full list of the 613 Mitzvot see the following site. Tracey R. Rich, "A List of the 613 Mitzvot (Commandments)," Judaism 101, http://www.jewfaq.org/613.htm.

not reap to the very edges of your field, or gather the gleanings of your harvest." (Leviticus 19:9 NRSV)
3. "Since there will never cease to be some in need on the earth, I therefore command you, 'Open your hand to the poor and needy neighbor in your land.'" (Deuteronomy 15:11)
4. "If there is among you anyone in need, a member of your community in any of your towns within the land that the Lord your God is giving you, do not be hard-hearted or tight-fisted toward your needy neighbor." (Deuteronomy 15:7)

Quiz 3 for Chapter 3

1-4. Describe in four ways how the *Enuma Elish's* creation epic differs from the divinely inspired Genesis account.

    1.

    2.

    3.

    4.

5-7. What are the three basic ways of interpreting Sacred Scripture? In answering this question include reference to *Divino Afflante Spiritu.*

    5.

    6.

    7.

8. According to Genesis, why are human beings of great value and fundamentally equal?

9. Describe two fundamental ways where the Jewish reverence for law influenced Western Civilization.

Chapter 4

Greek Civilization

Introduction

The second civilization that made a substantial contribution to Western Civilization were the Greeks. We will study Greek civilization by directing our attention to two of its principal and competing city states: Athens and Sparta. Tension between these two city states resulted in the Peloponnesian wars (431-404 BC), which Sparta won. In the 300s BC, the Northern Macedonian Alexander the Great united all of Greece under his rule.

The Greek City-States

Greek city-states began forming around 900 BC. A major factor that influenced this development is Greek geography. Greek lands are situated on a peninsula called the Balkan Peninsula that juts out into the Ionian Sea, Mediterranean Sea, Cretan Sea, and Thracian Sea. These various seas flow into and over Greek lands dividing the country up. The geographical divisions (determined by water, islands, plains, and highlands) influenced the Greek people to identify with small cities. Each city and its associated regions commanded loyalty from its people. Common laws, customs, rituals, philosophies, and gods bound the people together whose hub was a city. In time, there were hundreds of Greek city-states, each claiming loyalty from its citizens and with a distinct set of laws, customs, rituals, philosophies, and theologies. Some of the most powerful Greek city-states were Argos, Elis, Achaea, Sicyon, Corinth, Megara, Orchomenus, Thebes, Thessaly, Athens, and Sparta. Athens and Sparta emerged as the two most powerful of these city states. As we will study, they differed significantly from one another.[35]

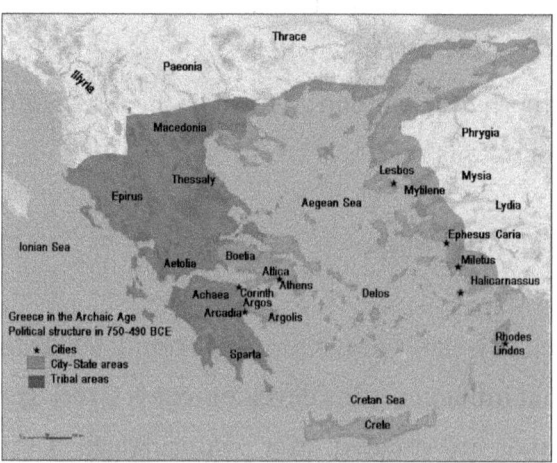

Greek City States (750-480 B.C.)[36]

---

[35] Raphael Sealey, *A History of the Greek City States, Ca. 700-338 B.C.* (Berkeley: University of California Press, 1976), 10-23.

[36] Map of the archaic period in Greece (750 – 480 BC).

Athens

In 510 BC, Athens distinguished itself from other Greek city-states by instituting a direct form of democratic governance. In a direct democracy, only possible on a small scale, the citizens and not elected officials decide the policies of the state. The wisdom of the Athenian experiment with democracy, limited only to free men, became a model for other states to follow.

Athenian reputation for wisdom was reflected in their patron goddess Athena. The goddess whom Athenians believed protected and guided their city was revered for her wisdom and reason. According to the Greek philosopher Plato (c. 427-347 BC), with reference to Homer, Athena's name is derived from Greek words meaning moral and divine intelligence.[37]

Prior to the establishment of Athenian democracy, the Athenians contributed another foundational concept for Western Civilization, the idea of a written down code of law that is universally applied to all. This is often referred to as the rule of law. The writer of Athens's first written code of law was Draco. Prior to Draco, Athens was ruled by a complex system of oral traditions that were not widely known

---

https://commons.wikimedia.org/wiki/File%3AArchaicGr.jpg

[37] Plato, "Cratylus," trans Benjamin Jowett, Ancient Texts, http://www.ancienttexts.org/library/greek/plato/cratylus.html

nor uniformly applied. Around 622 BC, Draco proposed a legal code that became incorporated into the first governing constitution of Athens.[38] Writing down laws enabled them to be more widely known, at least to those who could read, and made them capable of being applied equally. Another means which Draco established to ensure equal justice for many was a jury system by which the guilt of the accused was

---

[38] Aristotle, *Athenian Constitution*, trans. Sir Frederic G. Kenyon, sec. 2, no. 41, The Internet Classics Archive, http://classics.mit.edu/Aristotle/athenian_const.2.2.html. "This, however, took place at a later date; at the time of which we are speaking the people, having secured the control of the state, established the constitution which exists at the present day. Pythodorus was Archon at the time, but the democracy seems to have assumed the supreme power with perfect justice, since it had effected its own return by its own exertions. This was the eleventh change which had taken place in the constitution of Athens. The first modification of the primaeval condition of things was when Ion and his companions brought the people together into a community, for then the people was first divided into the four tribes, and the tribe-kings were created. Next, and first after this, having now some semblance of a constitution, was that which took place in the reign of Theseus, consisting in a slight deviation from absolute monarchy. After this came the constitution formed under Draco, when the first code of laws was drawn up. The third was that which followed the civil war, in the time of Solon; from this the democracy took its rise."; Edwin Carawan, *Rhetoric and the Law of Draco* (Oxford: Oxford University Press, 1998), 1.

Chapter 4: Greek Civilization

determined by the majority vote of a jury.[39]

Even though during Draco's life his laws were recognized as a significant advance in the application of justice in a fair manner, later Athenians viewed Draco's law code as excessively severe, hence our term Draconian. According to the early Greek historian Plutarch (c. 46-120 AD), echoing the Athenian Demades' (c. 380-318 BC) complaint that "Draco's laws were written in blood," Draco's laws were severe since the penalty for many infractions was death.[40]

Building upon and moderating Draco's code of law and the Athenian constitution, the Athenian ruler (*archon*) Solon (c. 638-558 BC) prepared the way for Athens's experiment with democracy.[41] During the fourth century BC, Greeks began to view Solon as the father of Athenian democracy. However, as demonstrated by V. Ehrenberg, Solon never intended to institute a democracy.[42] Even so, it can be argued, that Solon's political, economic, and constitutional reforms created necessary conditions for a democracy to take root. The following are excerpts from Plutarch's history of Solon.

---

[39] Carawan, *Rhetoric and the Law of Draco*, 2.

[40] Carawan, *Rhetoric and the Law of Draco*, 2.

[41] V. Ehrenberg, *From Solon to Socrates: Greek History and Civilization during the 6th and 5th Centuries BC* (London: Routledge, 1973), 64-65.

[42] Ibid., 67.

~ Plutarch on Solon ~

First, then, he repealed all Draco's laws, except those concerning homicide, because they were too severe, and the punishment too great; for death was appointed for almost all offences, insomuch that those that were convicted of idleness were to die, and those that stole a cabbage or an apple to suffer even as villains that committed sacrilege or murder. So that Demades, in after time, was thought to have said very happily, that Draco's laws were written not with ink but blood; and he himself, being once asked why he made death the punishment of most offences, replied, "Small ones deserve that, and I have no higher for the greater crimes."[43]

One of Athens's most notable fourth-century democratic leaders was Pericles (c. 495-429 BC). He was born a few years before the Greek city states prevented the Persian Empire from overtaking Greek lands during the Greco-Persian War (499-449). Pericles governed Athens as a statesman and as a military leader. The time of Pericles' rule is often called the Athenian Golden Age. During this golden era, Pericles promoted Athenian democratic values and aimed at creating an empire with Athens as its center.

---

[43] Plutarch, "Solon," trans. John Dryden, The Internet Classics Archives, http://classics.mit.edu/Plutarch/solon.html

Chapter 4: Greek Civilization

The Athenian Golden Age is comparable to the Renaissance in that under Pericles rule architects, sculptors, playwrights, and intellectuals received substantial funding. Since Athens was not a dictatorship but a democracy, albeit limited to free men, Pericles needed to provide motivation other than fear for its citizens to actively support their democratic life. This was especially important when it came to Athenian military service. Pericles successfully provided this motivation by instilling into Athenians a sense of civic duty defined by civic virtue that concerns the common good and not only the individual good.

Near the end of Pericles' life, his ambitions for Athens to dominate Peloponnese, the peninsula of southern Greece, caused tension with other city-states, principally with Sparta. The friction resulted in the Peloponnesian War (431-404 BC). The Peloponnesian War between Athens and the Spartan Peloponnesian League ended with Sparta as the victor. During the war, the population of Athens was decimated by a terrible plague. Desiring a scapegoat, Athens's citizens turned against Pericles and removed him from office.[44]

A few years after the Peloponnesian war[45] ended with

---

[44] Donald Kagan, *Pericles of Athens and the Birth of Democracy* (New York: The Free Press, 1991), 1-10.

[45] "The Alliances of the Peloponnesian War," map, https://commons.wikimedia.org/wiki/File%3APeloponnesian

Athens as the loser in 404 BC, another scapegoat was chosen by the Athenians, this time a philosopher, the great Athenian philosopher Socrates. Socrates was placed on trial, found guilty of corrupting the youth, and ordered by Athens to commit suicide. In 399 BC, he complied with his state's orders, drank the hemlock given to him, and died. His death and his philosophical ideas have left a deep impression on Western Civilization. One contribution for which he is well known is the Socratic Method.

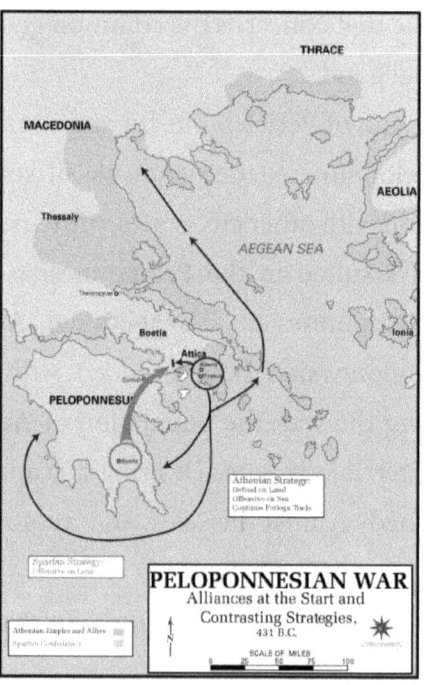

Below, is an example of this method of education, which consists of teaching by raising questions instead of giving

_war_alliances_431_BC.png

answers.[46]

PERSONS OF THE DIALOGUE: Meno, Socrates, A Slave of Meno (Boy), Anytus.

MENO: Can you tell me, Socrates, whether virtue is acquired by teaching or by practice; or if neither by teaching nor by practice, then whether it comes to man by nature, or in what other way?

SOCRATES: O Meno, there was a time when the Thessalians were famous among the other Hellenes only for their riches and their riding; but now, if I am not mistaken, they are equally famous for their wisdom, especially at Larisa, which is the native city of your friend Aristippus. And this is Gorgias' doing; for when he came there, the flower of the Aleuadae, among them your admirer Aristippus, and the other chiefs of the Thessalians, fell in love with his wisdom. And he has taught you the habit of answering questions in a grand and bold style, which becomes those who know, and is the style in which he himself answers all comers; and any Hellene who likes may ask him anything. How different is our lot! my dear Meno. Here at Athens there is a dearth of the

---

[46] Plato, "Meno," trans. Benjamin Jowett, *Project Gutenberg* http://www.gutenberg.org/files/1643/1643-h/1643-h.htm

commodity, and all wisdom seems to have emigrated from us to you. I am certain that if you were to ask any Athenian whether virtue was natural or acquired, he would laugh in your face, and say: 'Stranger, you have far too good an opinion of me, if you think that I can answer your question. For I literally do not know what virtue is, and much less whether it is acquired by teaching or not.' And I myself, Meno, living as I do in this region of poverty, am as poor as the rest of the world; and I confess with shame that I know literally nothing about virtue; and when I do not know the 'quid' of anything how can I know the 'quale'? How, if I knew nothing at all of Meno, could I tell if he was fair, or the opposite of fair; rich and noble, or the reverse of rich and noble? Do you think that I could?

MENO: No, indeed. But are you in earnest, Socrates, in saying that you do not know what virtue is? And am I to carry back this report of you to Thessaly?

SOCRATES: Not only that, my dear boy, but you may say further that I have never known of anyone else who did, in my judgment.

MENO: Then you have never met Gorgias when he was at Athens?

SOCRATES: Yes, I have.

MENO: And did you not think that he knew?

SOCRATES: I have not a good memory, Meno, and therefore I cannot now tell what I thought of him at the time. And I dare say that he did know, and that you know what he said: please, therefore, to remind me of what he said; or, if you would rather, tell me your own view; for I suspect that you and he think much alike.

MENO: Very true.

SOCRATES: Then as he is not here, never mind him, and do you tell me: By the gods, Meno, be generous, and tell me what you say that virtue is; for I shall be truly delighted to find that I have been mistaken, and that you and Gorgias do really have this knowledge; although I have been just saying that I have never found anybody who had.

MENO: There will be no difficulty, Socrates, in answering your question. Let us take first the virtue of a man—he should know how to administer the state, and in the administration of it to benefit his friends and harm his enemies; and he must also be careful not to suffer harm himself. A woman's virtue, if you wish to know about that, may also be easily described: her duty is to order her house, and keep what is indoors, and obey her husband. Every age, every condition of life, young or old, male or female, bond or free, has a different virtue: there are virtues numberless, and no lack of definitions of them; for virtue is relative to the actions and ages of each of us in all that we do. And the same may be said of vice, Socrates.

SOCRATES: How fortunate I am, Meno! When I ask you for one virtue, you present me with a swarm of them, which are in your keeping. Suppose that I carry on the figure of the swarm, and ask of you, What is the nature of the bee? and you answer that there are many kinds of bees, and I reply: But do bees differ as bees, because there are many and different kinds of them; or are they not rather to be distinguished by some other quality, as for example beauty, size, or shape? How would you answer me?

MENO: I should answer that bees do not differ from one another, as bees.

SOCRATES: And if I went on to say: That is what I desire to know, Meno; tell me what is the quality in which they do not differ, but are all alike; would you be able to answer?

MENO: I should.

Chapter 4: Greek Civilization

SOCRATES: And so of the virtues, however many and different they may be, they have all a common nature which makes them virtues; and on this he who would answer the question, 'What is virtue?' would do well to have his eye fixed: Do you understand?

MENO: I am beginning to understand; but I do not as yet take hold of the question as I could wish.

SOCRATES: When you say, Meno, that there is one virtue of a man, another of a woman, another of a child, and so on, does this apply only to virtue, or would you say the same of health, and size, and strength? Or is the nature of health always the same, whether in man or woman?

MENO: I should say that health is the same, both in man and woman.

SOCRATES: And is not this true of size and strength? If a woman is strong, she will be strong by reason of the same form and of the same strength subsisting in her which there is in the man. I mean to say that strength, as strength, whether of man or woman, is the same. Is there any difference?

MENO: I think not.

SOCRATES: And will not virtue, as virtue, be the same, whether in a child or in a grown-up person, in a woman or in a man?

MENO: I cannot help feeling, Socrates, that this case is different from the others.

SOCRATES: But why? Were you not saying that the virtue of a man was to order a state, and the virtue of a woman was to order a house?

MENO: I did say so. Such is the inference.

SOCRATES: And they surely would not have been good in the same way, unless their virtue had been the same?

MENO: They would not.

SOCRATES: Then now that the sameness of all virtue has been proven, try and remember what you and Gorgias say that virtue is.

MENO: Will you have one definition of them all?
SOCRATES: That is what I am seeking.

Sparta

Xenophon (431-354 BC) was a pupil of Socrates and fellow Athenian who also was punished by the Athenians by being exiled from his city-state. He sought refuge in Sparta. There he recorded Spartan life which, unlike Athens, did not value democracy. Instead, Sparta was governed in a militaristic manner with a strict hierarchy. After defeating the Athenians in the Peloponnesian War (431-404 BC), Sparta remained a dominant power in Greece. They maintained their influence even under Alexander the Great's Greek Empire. Spartan power came to an end when the Roman Empire sacked the city-state of Corinth in 146 BC and then subdued the other Greek city-states. The Sack of Corinth occurred during the Achaean War between the Greek Achaean League and the Roman Empire.[47]

The following excerpts from Xenophon on Sparta help us determine how Sparta differed from Athens and the rest of what Xenophon calls "Hellas":

> But when we turn to Lycurgus, instead of leaving it to each member of the state privately to appoint a slave to be his son's tutor, he set over the young Spartans a public guardian, the *Paidonomos* or "pastor," to give them his

---

[47] Nigel Wilson, *Encyclopedia of Ancient Greece* (New York: Routledge, 2010), 5-6, 187.

proper title, with complete authority over them. This guardian was selected from those who filled the highest magistracies. He had authority to hold musters of the boys, and as their overseer, in case of any misbehavior, to chastise severely. The legislator further provided his pastor with a body of youths in the prime of life, and bearing whips, to inflict punishment when necessary, with this happy result that in Sparta modesty and obedience ever go hand in hand, nor is there lack of either.

...

Instead of softening their feet with shoe or sandal [as the Athenians and other Greek city-states do], his rule was to make them hardy through going barefoot. This habit, if practiced, would, as he believed, enable them to scale heights more easily and clamber down precipices with less danger. In fact, with his feet so trained the young Spartan would leap and spring and run faster unshod than another shod in the ordinary way.

...

Instead of making them effeminate with a variety of clothes, his rule was to habituate them to a single garment the whole year through, thinking that so they would be better prepared to withstand the variations of heat and cold.

Again, as regards food, according to his regulation the Eiren, or head of the flock, must see that his messmates gathered to the club meal, with such moderate food as to avoid that heaviness which is engendered by repletion, and yet not to remain altogether unacquainted with the pains of penurious living. His belief was that by such training in boyhood they would be better able when occasion demanded to continue toiling on an empty stomach. They would be all the fitter, if the word of command were given, to remain on the stretch for a long time without extra dieting. The craving for luxuries would be less, the readiness to take any victual set before them greater, and, in general, the regime would be found healthier. Under it he thought the lads would increase in stature and shape into finer men, since, as he maintained, a dietary which gave suppleness to the limbs must be more conducive to both ends than one which added thickness to the bodily parts by feeding.

...

I ought, as it seems to me, not to omit some remark on the subject of boy attachments, it being a topic in close connection with that of boyhood and the training of boys.

...

Furthermore, [in contrast with Athens and other Greek city-states] in his [the Spartan ruler Lycurgus's] desire to implant in their youthful souls a root of modesty he imposed upon these bigger boys a special rule. In the very streets they were to keep their two hands within the folds of the cloak; they were to walk in silence and without turning their heads to gaze, now here, now there, but rather to keep their eyes fixed upon the ground before them. And hereby it would seem to be proved conclusively that, even in the matter of quiet bearing and sobriety, the masculine type may claim greater strength than that which we attribute to the nature of women. At any rate, you might sooner expect a stone image to find voice than one of those Spartan youths; to divert the eyes of some bronze stature were less difficult. And as to quiet bearing, no bride ever stepped in bridal bower with more natural modesty. Note them when they have reached the public table. The plainest answer to the question asked—that is all you need expect to hear from their lips.

...

With regard to those who have already passed the vigor of early manhood, and on whom the highest magistracies henceforth devolve, there is a like contrast. In Hellas [Athens and on Greek city-states] generally we find that at this age the need of further attention to physical strength is removed, although the imposition of military service continues. But Lycurgus [the Spartan law maker] made it customary for that section of his citizens to regard hunting as the highest honor suited to their age; albeit, not to the exclusion of any public duty. And his aim was that they might be equally able to undergo the fatigues of war with those in the prime of early manhood.

...

The above is a fairly exhaustive statement of the institutions traceable to the legislation of Lycurgus in connection with the successive stages of a citizen's life. It remains that I should endeavour to describe the style of living which he established for the whole body, irrespective of age. It will be understood that, when Lycurgus first came to deal with the question, the Spartans like the rest of the Hellenes, used to mess privately at home. Tracing more than half the current misdemeanors to this custom, he was determined to drag his people out of holes and corners into the broad daylight, and so [unlike Athens and other Greek city-states] he invented the public mess-rooms. Whereby he expected at any rate to minimize the transgression of orders.

...

There are yet other customs in Sparta which Lycurgus instituted in opposition to those of the rest of Hellas [Athens and other Greek city-states], and the following among them. We all know that in the generality of states every one devotes his full energy to the business of making money: one man as a tiller of the soil, another as a mariner, a third as a merchant, whilst others depend on various arts to earn a living. But at Sparta Lycurgus forbade his freeborn citizens to have anything whatsoever to do with the concerns of money-making. As freemen, he enjoined upon them to regard as their concern exclusively those activities upon which the foundations of civic liberty are based.

…

But to proceed. We are all aware that there is no state in the world in which greater obedience is shown to magistrates, and to the laws themselves, than Sparta. But, for my part, I am disposed to think that Lycurgus could never have attempted to establish this healthy condition, until he had first secured the unanimity of the most powerful members of the state. I infer this for the following reasons. In other states the leaders in rank and influence do not even desire to be thought to fear the magistrates. Such a thing they would regard as in itself a symbol of servility. In Sparta, on the contrary, the stronger a man is the more readily does he bow before constituted authority. And indeed, they magnify themselves on their humility, and on a prompt obedience, running, or at any rate not crawling with laggard step, at the word of command. Such an example of eager discipline, they are persuaded, set by themselves, will not fail to be followed by the rest. And this is precisely what has taken place. It is reasonable to suppose that it was these same noblest members of the state who combined to lay the foundation of the *ephorate*, after they had come to the conclusion themselves, that of all the blessings which a state, or an army, or a household, can enjoy, obedience is the greatest. Since, as they could not but reason, the greater the power with which men fence about authority, the greater the fascination it will exercise upon the mind of the citizen, to the enforcement of obedience.

…

Accordingly the *ephors* are competent to punish whomsoever they choose; they have power to exact fines on the spur of the moment; they have power to depose magistrates in mid-career—nay, actually to imprison them and bring them to trial on the capital charge. Entrusted with these vast powers, they do not, as do the rest of states [Athens and the other Greek city-states], allow the magistrates elected to exercise authority as they like, right through the year of office; but, in the style rather of despotic monarchs, or presidents of the games, at the first symptom of an offence against the law they inflict chastisement without warning and without hesitation.

…

Lycurgus laid it down as law that the king [once again in contrast with Athenian democracy] shall offer in behalf of the state all public sacrifices, as being himself of divine descent, and whithersoever the state shall despatch her armies the king shall take the lead.[48]

---

[48] Xenophon, "The Polity of the Athenians and the Lacedaemonians," trans. H. G. Dakyns, Project Gutenberg, http://www.gutenberg.org/files/1178/1178-h/1178-h.htm

Alexander the Great and the Greek Empire

Alexander the Great's Empire in 323 BC[49]

In fourth century BC, the Northern Macedonian king, Philip II (382–336 BC) successfully dominated the Greek city-states and planned to replace the Persian Empire. Fulfilling his father's dreams, Alexander the Great (356-323 BC), tutored by Aristotle, successfully created a vast Greek Empire that defeated and replaced the Persian Empire.[50] Because of Alexander's conquests, Greek art, literature, and

---

[49] Thomas Lessman, "Alexander's empire was the largest state of its time, covering approximately 5.2 million square km, The Empire of Alexander the Great in 323 BC," map, https://commons.wikimedia.org/wiki/File%3AAlexander-Empire_323bc.jpg

[50] Robin Osborne, *Greek History* (Routledge: London, 2004), 125-132.

Chapter 4: Greek Civilization

philosophy made a lasting and significant impression on Western Civilization.[51] Alexander's zeal to extend Greek culture caused him to invade India.

Shortly after his attempted conquest of India, he died. He was only 32 years old. As explained in the previous chapter, after his death his empire was divided up between four powerful men: Cassander, Lysimachus, Ptolemy, and Seleucus I Nicator.

Quiz 4 for Chapter 4

1. What is a geographic explanation for the formation of Greek city-states?

2-5. Where was Draco from and around what time did he live? With respect to law, what foundational concept did Draco contribute to Western Civilization? Finally, why does the English word Draconian have a negative connotation to it?

2.

3.

---

[51] Philip Freeman, *Alexander the Great* (New York: Simon & Schuster, 2011), 323.

4.

5.

6-9. Where was Solon from and around what time did he live? With respect to law how did he differ from Draco? What is he considered as the founder of?

6.

7.

8.

9.

10-13. Where was Pericles from and around what time did he live? What political system did he actively promote? In order for this political system to function effectively, what means did he encourage in the citizens of the city-state in which he lived?

10.

11.

12.

Chapter 4: Greek Civilization

13.

14-15. What two wars did the Athenian Golden Age fall between? Who won the second war?

14.

15.

16-19. Where was Socrates from and around what time did he live? How did he die and why?

16.

17.

18.

19.

20-27. Choose one of the following.

A. Using the *Meno* as a guide, write at least 8 sentences of a dialogue between a teacher and a student.

20.

21.

22.

23.

24.

25.

26.

27.

B. Contrast Athens with Sparta in four ways.

20-21.

22-23.

24-25.

26-27.

Chapter 5

Greek Culture

Introduction

In this chapter, we will continue studying the Greeks through their culture: religion, literature, philosophy, art, and theatre. The various aspects of Greek culture made a lasting and deep impression on Western Civilization principally, as seen in the previous chapter, because Alexander the Great established a vast empire held together by a Greek way of life that the Romans looked up to after they replaced the Greeks and established their own empire.

Representing the Roman positive approach to Greek culture, Virgil (70-19 BC) wrote:

> Others [the Greeks] ... will hammer out bronze that breathes with more delicacy than us, draw out living features from marble: plead their causes better, trace with instruments the movement of the skies, and tell the rising of the constellations. Remember, Roman, it is for you to rule the nations with your power (that will be your skill) to crown peace with law, to spare the conquered,

and subdue the proud.⁵²

Greek Gods

In his work called *Theogony* the Greek poet Hesiod (c. 750-650 BC) describes the origins of the Gods and traces their genealogies. Below, in verse form, is his description of how the Gods came to be. Notice how Chaos existed before the Gods and that Chaos also had a beginning. What Hesiod means by this and what Chaos is is not clear. What is clear is that, contrary to the book of Genesis, Hesiod did not claim that a creative intelligence is at the origin of all things that were created out of nothing. As explained by Apostolos N. Athanassakis, rather, "It is a physical world born not *ex nihilo* but *ex ignoto*, 'from the unknown.'"⁵³

The first fundamental realities that Hesiod names as coming into existence after Chaos, or along with Chaos, are

---

⁵² Virgil, *Aeneid*, Book VI, 808-853, trans. A.S. Kline, Poetry in Translation, http://www.poetryintranslation.com/PITBR/Latin/VirgilAeneidVI.htm# Virgil's *Aeneid* was modeled after Homer's *Illiad* and *Odyssey*. It tells the story of the Trojan Aeneas who landed on the shore of Italian lands. Aeneas was considered by the Romans as the primordial founder of Rome and the ancestor of Romulus and Remus.

⁵³ Apostolos N. Athanassakis, *Hesiod: Theogony, Works and Days, Shield*, second ed. (Baltimore: John Hopkins University Press, 2004), 7.

Chapter 5: Greek Culture

earth (Gaia), the abyss (Tartarus), and love (Eros). In her virgin state Gaia gives birth to the starry heavens (Uranus), the sea (Pontus), and the hills. Earth, the heavens, the mountains and the sea are for Hesiod the first four elements of the world. Chaos also is responsible for giving rise to four realities: darkness, night, light, and day.[54] After the earth experiences a "sweet union of love" with her virgin born, heavenly son by inviting him "to cover her on every side," she gives birth to the Titans: Oceanus, Coeus, Crius, Hyperion, Iapetus, Theia, Rhea, Themis, Mnemosyne, Phoebe, and Tethys. Finally, she gives birth to last Titan, Cronos, who becomes the Titan's leader.[55]

~ Hesiod's *Theogony* ~

Hail, children of Zeus! Grant lovely song and celebrate the holy race of the deathless gods who are forever, those that were born of Earth and starry Heaven and gloomy Night and them that briny Sea did rear. Tell how at the first gods and earth came to be, and rivers, and the

---

[54] Apostolos N. Athanassakis, *Hesiod: Theogony, Works and Days, Shield*, 2nd ed. (Baltimore: John Hopkins University Press, 2004), 1-8.
[55] Hesiod, "Theogony," 104, Perseus Digital Library, http://www.perseus.tufts.edu/hopper/text?doc=Perseus%3Atext%3A1999.01.0130%3Acard%3D104

boundless sea with its raging swell, and the gleaming stars, and the wide heaven above, and the gods who were born of them, givers of good things, and how they divided their wealth, and how they shared their honors amongst them, and also how at the first they took many-folded Olympus. These things declare to me from the beginning, you Muses who dwell in the house of Olympus, and tell me which of them first came to be. In truth at first Chaos came to be, but next wide-bosomed Earth, the ever-sure foundation of all the deathless ones who hold the peaks of snowy Olympus, and dim Tartarus in the depth of the wide-pathed Earth [Gaia], and Eros (Love), fairest among the deathless gods, who unnerves the limbs and overcomes the mind and wise counsels of all gods and all men within them. From Chaos came forth Erebus [darkness] and black Night [Nyx]; but of Night were born Aether [upper air] and Day [Hemera], whom she conceived and bore from union in love with Erebus. And Earth first bore starry Heaven [Uranus], equal to herself, to cover her on every side, and to be an ever-sure abiding-place for the blessed gods. And she brought forth long hills, graceful haunts of the goddess Nymphs who dwell amongst the glens of the hills. She bore also the fruitless deep with his raging swell, Pontus, [sea] without sweet union of love. But afterwards she lay with Heaven and bore deep-swirling Oceanus, Coeus and Crius and Hyperion and Iapetus, Theia and Rhea, Themis and

Mnemosyne and gold-crowned Phoebe and lovely Tethys. After them was born Cronos the wily, youngest and most terrible of her children, and he hated his lusty sire.[56]

In the following verses, Hesiod describes Mother Earth's giving birth to one-eyed giant creatures called Cyclopes and three other even mightier creatures each with a hundred hands and fifty heads. Hating these monster children, Mother Earth calls upon her Titan son Cronus to punish her husband Uranus. Cronus agrees and hides with a sickle while his father spreads "himself full upon her."[57] Seizing upon this opportune moment, Cronus castrates his father and cast his father's organs into the sea, causing it to foam. Soon after, Aphrodite, the goddess of love, is born out of the sea's foam.

The Florentine Renaissance artist J. Sandro Botticelli (1445-1510) depicted the birth of Aphrodite by reinterpreting the myth within a Christian context. The angelic figures blowing a modest looking Aphrodite across the waters represent angels introducing the Blessed Mother who

---

[56] Hesiod, "Theogony," 104, Perseus Digital Library, http://www.perseus.tufts.edu/hopper/text?doc=Perseus%3Atext%3A1999.01.0130%3Acard%3D104

[57] Hesiod, "Theogony," 173, Perseus Digital Library, http://www.perseus.tufts.edu/hopper/text?doc=Perseus%3Atext%3A1999.01.0130%3Acard%3D173

is bringing divine love into the world.⁵⁸

Botticelli's *Birth of Venus*⁵⁹

Cronos has relations with the Goddess Rhea who bears him beautiful children. Cronos swallows each of his children

---

⁵⁸ H.W. Janson, and Anthony F. Janson, *History of Art*, (New York: Harry N. Abrams, 2001), 421; Aphrodite was the Greek Goddess of love. According to one version of a Greek myth, after Cronus, son of Gaia (earth goddess) and Uranus (sky god), cut off Uranus' genitals and cast them into the sea, foam rose and out of the foam Aphrodite was born. In accordance with her origins, her name means "foam-arisen." She arrived on land by floating on scallop shell. Robert Graves, *The Greek Myths* (London: Penguin Books, 1960), 49.

⁵⁹ "Sandro Botticelli's "The Birth of Venus," Uffizi Gallery, Florence, http://commons.wikimedia.org/wiki/File%3ALa_ nascita_ di_Venere_(Botticelli).jpg.

Chapter 5: Greek Culture

as they come "forth from the womb to his mother's knees with this intent, that no other of the proud sons of Heaven should hold the kingly office amongst the deathless gods."[60] In grief, Rhea appeals to her parents Earth and Heaven who advise her, before she gives birth to her next son Zeus, to wrap a big stone in swaddling, baby clothes and present that to her husband to eat, which he does. When Zeus is strong enough, he drives his father from his throne and rules the gods in his place.

Zeus's authority is itself challenged by another god when Prometheus steals fire from Zeus and gives it to men. Zeus punishes Prometheus by binding him to a mountain where he daily faces an eagle. During the day the eagle eats Prometheus' liver. During the night, the liver grows back.[61] Eventually, Zeus decides to wipe out the human race, which has become increasingly violent after being given the power of fire. In punishment, he sends down a torrential downpour that quickly inundates the whole earth in water. Living among the men is Prometheus's son, Deucalion. As told by Lucian of Samosata (c. 125-180 AD) in *The Syrian Goddess*:

> They were extremely violent and committed lawless

---

[60] Hesiod, "Theogony," 453, Perseus Digital Library, http://www.perseus.tufts.edu/hopper/text?doc=Perseus%3Atext%3A1999.01.0130%3Acard%3D104

[61] Chapter 2, book 1.

deeds, for they neither kept oaths nor welcomed strangers nor spared suppliants. As punishment for these offenses the great disaster came upon them. Suddenly the earth poured forth a flood of water. Heavy rains fell, rivers rushed down in torrents, and the sea rose on high, until everything became water, and all the people perished. Deucalion alone among the men was left for the second race because of his prudence and piety. This was the manner of this salvation: He embarked his children and his wives into a great ark which he possessed and he himself went in. As he boarded, pigs and horses, species of lions, snakes and every kind of creature that grazes on earth came to him, all of them in pairs. He welcomed all, and none harmed him. Instead, from some divine source, there was great friendship among them, and in a single ark all sailed as long as the flood prevailed. This, then, is the story which Greeks tell about Deucalion.[62]

According to Apollodorus of Athens (180-120 BC), for nine days and nights Deucalion's ark floats safely in the flood until it comes to rest on a mountain top. After the rain stops and the flood waters subside, Deucalion and his family disembark and pray to Zeus asking him for men to be created.

---

[62] Marvin W. Meyer, *The Ancient Mysteries: A Sourcebook of Sacred Texts* (Philadelphia: University of Pennsylvania Press, 1999), 133-134.

Following Zeus' instructions Deucalion and his wife Pyrrha throw stones over their heads. Pyrrha's stones turns into women, while Deucalion's changes into men. The first son he has with Pyrrha, he names Hellen. Hellen becomes the father of the Greek people.[63]

As is evident, this account of a great flood bears similarities with the biblical account in *Genesis*. The Sumerian *Epic of Gilgamesh* (c. 2100 BC) is another ancient text that also describes a flood caused by Gods in which a man named Utnapishtim builds an ark and survives. This epic is but one of many flood stories from ancient cultures. The Catholic philosopher Joseph Pieper in explaining this phenomenon from a faith perspective refers to the Augustinian concept of an original revelation. He writes:

> And yet it would be an inappropriate narrowing of the true state of affairs to see 'sacred tradition' realized only in the realm of biblical and Christian doctrine. It is narrow-minded to define tradition, taken as process as act, as nothing more than 'the ecclesiastical proclamation of belief, which began with the Apostles…and was continued by their successors with the same authority.' Such a limitation of the term is even theologically question-

---

[63] Apollodorus, *Gods and Heroes of the Greeks: The Library of Apollodorus*, trans. Michael Simpson (Amherst: University of Massachusetts Press, 1976), 32-33.

able. Can one dispute so simply the claim of the mythical tradition in the pre- and non-Christian realm to preserve through the ages knowledge which equally comes down from a divine source-especially insofar as we are convinced that there existed, long before the 'Apostles,' something like an 'original revelation'? This last concept, which we have mentioned before, does not have an especially high standing in the current discussion, if indeed it is mentioned at all. It has been at home in Christian theology, however, since the earliest times and it will always recur to memory as something indispensable. The concept of 'original revelation,' betokens that at the beginning of history an event took place of a divine speech directed especially to 'the' man, that is to *all* men, and that time has entered into the sacred tradition of all peoples-in their myths, that is-and is preserved and present there, more or less recognizably. Augustine, in his latework the *Retractiones*, formulated this thought-admittedly in a way that is all too easy to understand and has in fact often been misunderstood: 'The very thing which is now called the 'Christian religion' existed among the ancients. Indeed it has never been absent since the beginning of the human race, until Christ appeared in the flesh. That was when the true religion, which already existed, began to be called the

'Christian religion.'"⁶⁴

Greek Literature

Along with works on the gods, such as the mentioned above Hesiod's *Theogony*, Greek literature also included epic poetry, lyric poetry, and plays. Two of the most significant epic works were both written by Homer (c. 600s BC). These epics are the *Iliad* and the *Odyssey*.

Epic Poetry

The *Iliad* describes the Trojan War between the Trojans and Greeks that erupted after the Trojan man, Paris, stole an exquisitely beautiful woman called Helen, Queen of Sparta, married to the Spartan King Menelaus. Helen, feeling remorseful, reproaches Paris for his evil deed by saying, "would that you had fallen rather by the hand of that brave man who was my husband. You used to brag that you were a better man with hands and spear than Menelaus. Go, but I then, and challenge him again - but I should advise you not to do so, for if you are foolish enough to meet him in single combat, you will soon all die by his spear."⁶⁵

---

⁶⁴ Josef Pieper, *Tradition Concept and Claim*, trans. E. Christian Kopff (Wilmington: ISI Books, 2008), 50-51.

⁶⁵ Homer, *The Iliad*, trans. Samuel Butler, book III, The

Unashamed Paris responds, "Wife, do not vex me with your reproaches. This time, with the help of Minerva, Menelaus has vanquished me; another time I may myself be victor, for I too have gods that will stand by me. Come, let us lie down together and make friends. Never yet was I so passionately enamored of you as at this moment - not even when I first carried you off from Lacedaemon and sailed away with you - not even when I had converse with you upon the couch of love in the island of Cranae was I so enthralled by desire of you as now."[66]

These words persuade Helen to allow Paris to lead her "towards the bed,"[67] a bed that symbolizes the proximate cause of a terrible war. The remote cause of the war was due to a Golden Apple from Eris, goddess of strife, which the Goddess Aphrodite won in a beauty contest among the Goddesses. The judge of the beauty contest was none other than Paris, chosen by Zeus. In exchange for choosing her as the most beautiful of the Goddesses, Aphrodite rewards Paris by causing the married woman Helen to become infatuated with him.[68]

Internet Classics Archive, http://classics.mit.edu/Homer/iliad.3.iii.html

[66] Homer, *The Iliad*, book III.

[67] Homer, *The Iliad*, book III.

[68] Lucian, "The Dialogues of the Gods," Sacred Texts, http://www.sacred-texts.com/cla/luc/wl1/wl127.htm; Stasinus of

In describing certain events of the Trojan war, the *Iliad* revolves around the Greek hero Achilles who, according to legend, is invulnerable from being wounded except for his heel.[69] According to Greek mythology, knowing of this vulnerability, Paris kills Achilles by shooting him in the heel, hence the term Achilles heel. The *Odyssey* takes place after the city of Troy has fallen to the Greeks. It describes the journey back home from the Trojan war of the Greek warrior-hero Odysseus. He is traveling to his kingdom of Ithaca in order to be reunited with his wife Penelope.

Lyric Poetry

Another major form of Greek literature was poetry written in lyric form. In other words, often composed to be sung and at times accompanied by a stringed instrument called a lyre. At other times, this poetry was accompanied by a wind instrument called an *aulos*. Still other ancient Greek poetry categorized as lyric may have been sung but were not accom-

---

Cyprus, "The Epic Cycle," trans. Gregory Nagy, University of Houston, http://www.uh.edu/ ~cldue/texts/epiccycle.html

[69] Statius, "Achilleid," trans. J.H. Mozley, bk. 1a., http://www.theoi.com/Text/StatiusAchilleid1A.html. The following source is cited. Statius, Thebaid, Achilleid. Translated by Mozley, J H. Loeb Classical Library Volumes. Cambridge, MA, Harvard University Press; London, William Heinemann Ltd. 1928.

panied by a musical instrument.[70]

The foremost earliest Greek lyric poets (600s-400s BC) were recognized as follows: "Alcman, Alcaeus, Sappho, Stesichorus, Ibycus, Anacreon, Simonides, Bacchylides, and Pindar."[71] Below is a poem on death, and the longing of the human heart for lasting love that cannot be found in the loves of this world. It was composed by the woman poet Sappho (c. 630-570 BC).

Death

Death is an evil; so the Gods decree,

So they have judged, and such must rightly be Our mortal view; for they who dwell on high Had never lived, had it been good to die.

And so the poet's house should never know Of tears and lamentations any show;

Such things befit not us who deathless sing Of love and beauty, gladness and the spring.

---

[70] Douglas E. Gerber, A Companion to the Greek Lyric Poets (Leiden: Brill, 1997), 1.

[71] Gerber, *A Companion to the Greek Lyric Poets*, 2.

No hint of grief should mar the features of Our dreams of endless beauty, lasting love; For they reflect the joy inviolate, Eternal calm that fronts whatever fate.

Clëis, my darling, grieve no more, I pray! Let wandering winds thy sorrow bear away, And all our care; my daughter, let thy smile Shine through thy tears and gladden me the while.[72]

Greek Theatre

The ancient Greeks also wrote plays. Two very basic forms were tragedies, primarily serious plays drawn from myths, and comedies, based on funny, contemporary events. The most recognized playwrights from the 500s BC to the 200s BC were the Athenians Aeschylus (c. 525-456 BC), Sophocles (c. 496-406 BC) Euripides (c. 485-406 BC), Aristophanes (c. 450-385 BC), and Menander (c. 342-290 BC). The last two, Aristophanes and Menander, wrote comedies, while the other three wrote tragedies.[73] The majority of

---

[72] Sappho, "The Poems of Sappho: An Interpretative Rendition into English by John Myers O'Hara," Project Gutenberg, http://www.gutenberg.org/files/42166/42166-h/42166-h.htm#DEATH

[73] Graham Ley, *A Short Introduction to the Ancient Greek Theater*, Revised Edition (Chicago: University of Chicago, 2006), 1-5.

the plays composed by these Athenian playwrights were intended to be performed in a theatre built in honor of Dionysius, god of wine and fertility.

Greek Philosophy

A few of the most influential Greek philosophers were Thales (c. 624-546 BC) Democritus (c. 460-370 BC), the Sophists (400s BC), Parmenides (c. 515-460 BC), Heraclitus (c. 535-475 BC), Socrates (c. 470-399 BC), Plato (c. 427-347 BC), and Aristotle (c. 384-322 BC). Thales attempted to discover the most basic element of the cosmos. He concluded that it is water. Others disagreed with him, including Democritus who asserted that everything is made up of tiny odd shaped particles called atoms that are constantly colliding and recombining with one another.

The Sophists rejected the importance of speculating on what is most true and constant. Instead, they honed their skills and their pupils' skills at defeating an opponent in argument regardless of their position. Parmenides and Heraclitus were also not overly concerned with what element is most basic to the universe. However, they were deeply concerned with determining what aspect of reality is primary. Parmenides argued that oneness, and constancy is most real. Change, he thought, is an illusion. Heraclitus, on the other hand, held that change is not an illusion but is at the root of all reality.

Like Parmenides and Heraclitus, Socrates reflected upon ultimate reality. For this reason, he opposed the relativism of the Sophists. With his Socratic Method of questioning, he defended justice and related virtues as really existing. His pupil Plato recorded his master's teachings and further developed them with an idealistic philosophical approach. Plato in turn had a famous pupil, Aristotle, teacher of Alexander the Great. Aristotle moderated Plato's idealism with a realistic philosophy that more clearly affirms the reality of the world that we experience.

Although not a philosopher per se, the wisdom of the Greek physician Hippocrates (c. 460-370 BC) has also had a lasting impact of Western Civilization as evident in the well-known Hippocratic Oath. We will conclude this section with his Hippocratic Oath. Versions of this oath are still taken voluntarily by many medical students.

~ Hippocratic Oath ~

I swear by Apollo the Physician and Æsculapius, and I call Hygeia and Panacea and all the gods and goddesses to witness, that to the best of my power and judgment I will keep this oath and this contract; to wit—to hold him, who taught me this Art, equally dear to me as my parents; to share my substance with him; to supply him if he is in need of the necessaries of life; to regard his offspring in the same light as my own brothers, and to teach them this

Art, if they shall desire to learn it, without fee or contract; to impart the precepts, the oral teaching, and all the rest of the instruction to my own sons, and to the sons of my teacher, and to pupils who have been bound to me by contract, and who have been sworn according to the law of medicine.

I will adopt that system of regimen which, according to my ability and judgment, I consider for the benefit of my patients, and will protect them from everything noxious and injurious. I will give no deadly medicine to anyone, even if asked, nor will I give any such counsel, and similarly I will not give to a woman the means of procuring an abortion. With purity and with holiness I will pass my life and practice my art.... Into whatever houses I enter I will go into them for the benefit of the sick, keeping myself aloof from every voluntary act of injustice and corruption and lust. Whatever in the course of my professional practice, or outside of it, I see or hear which ought not to be spread abroad, I will not divulge, as reckoning that all such should be kept secret. If I continue to observe this oath and to keep it inviolate, may it be mine to enjoy life and the practice of the Art respected among all men forever. But should I violate this oath and forswear myself, may the reverse be my lot.[74]

---

[74] Charles Mcrae, *Fathers of Biology* (London: Percival & Co., 1890), 17, Project Gutenberg, http://www.gutenberg.org/files/

Chapter 5: Greek Culture   99

Greek Art

We will end this chapter with images of Greek art.

Geometric (c. 1050 BC to 700 BC)[75]

24456/24456-h/24456-h.htm

[75] In the order of their appearance above: 1) Marie-Lan Nguyen, "Geometric kyathos (or one-handled kantharos), Greek islands, c 850-800 BC," vase, http://commons.wikimedia.org/wiki/File%3AGeometric_kyathos_MBA_Rennes_D08-2-10.jpg, 2) Marie-Lan Nguyen, "Oinochoe, Geometric style, made in Cnossos c. 700-690 BC," vase, http://commons.wikimedia.org/wiki/File%3AOinochoe_Knossos_Louvre_AM778.jpg, and 3) Zde, "Late geometric Krater, Andros, Zagora, import of Evia, 750-690 BC. Archaeological Museum of Andros (Chora) M104," vase, http://commons.wikimedia.org/wiki/File%3AKrater_Late_geometric_AM_Andros_M104_090531.jpg.

Greek Orientalizing Art (c. 700 BC – 600 BC)[76]

---

[76] In the order of their appearance (above): Jastrow, "Prothesis scene: exposure of the dead and mourning. Detail. Late Geometric. From the Dipylon Cemetery in Athens, circa 750 BC," cemetery ceramic, http://commons.wikimedia.org/wiki/File%3AProthesis_Dipylon_Painter_Louvre_A517.jpg,
(below) 1) User:Bibi Saint-Pol, "Bild oil jug, Corinthian "animal frieze" style, ca. 580 BC," oil jug, http://commons.wikimedia.org/wiki/File%3ACorinthian_jug_animal_frieze_580_BC_Staatliche_Antikensammlung en.jpg, and 2) Jastrow, "Proto-Corinthian olpe with registers of lions, bulls, ibex and sphinxes, c. 640-30 BC, Louvre," vase, http://commons.wikimedia.org/wiki/File%3AOlpe_sphinx_Louvre_Cp10475.jpg.

Chapter 5: Greek Culture

Archaic (c. 800 BC – 480 BC)

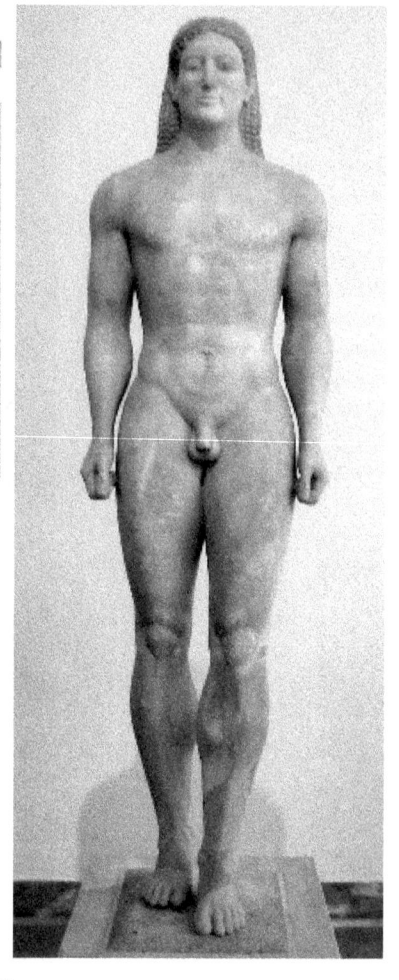

Male Kouros[77]

---

[77] "Kouros from Thebes," http://commons.wikimedia.org/wiki/File%3AKouros_from_thebes.jpg and "The Kroisos Kouros," in Parian marble, found in Anavyssos (Greece), dating from circa 530 BC, now exhibited at the National Archaeological Museum of Athens," http://commons.wikimedia.org/wiki/File%3AKouros_ anavissos.jpg.

Chapter 5: Greek Culture 103

Female Kore[78]

---

[78] Marsyas, "Peplos Kore, circa 530 BC, Athens, Acropolis Museum," statue, http://commons.wikimedia.org/wiki/File%3AACMA_679_Kore_1.JPG, and G.dallorto, "Painted kore reconstruction (Glyptothek, Munich)," http://commons.wikimedia.org/wiki/File:Istanbul_-_Museo_archeologico_-_Mostra_sul_colore_nell%27antichit%C3%A0_02__Foto_G._Dall%27Orto_28-5-2006.jpg#filehistory

Classical (c. 500-400)[79]

[79] Bibi Saint-Pol, "Heracles and Geryon on an Attic black-figured amphora with a thick layer of transparent gloss, c. 540 BC, now in the Munich State Collection of Antiquities," vase, http://commons.wikimedia.org/wiki/File%3AHerakles_Geryon_Staatliche_Antikensammlungen_1379.jpg, and Bibi Saint-Pol, "Heracles and Athena. Side A (red-figure) of an Attic bilingual amphora, 520–510 BC. From Vulci," vase, http://commons.wikimedia.org/wiki/File%3AAthena_Herakles_Staatliche_Antikensammlungen_2301_A.jpg.

Gods and Goddesses[80]

[80] Bib Saint-Pol, "So-called "Aphrodite Braschi", free copy (1st century BC) after a votive statue of Praxitele in Cnidus "Aphrodite of Cnidus" type, ca. 350–340 BC).," http://commons.wikimedia.org/wiki/File%3AAphrodite_Braschi_Glyptothek_Munich_258.jpg, and Pellegrini, "Bronze Sculpture, thought to be either Poseidon or Zeus," c. 460 BC, National Archaeological Museum, Athens. This masterpiece of classical sculpture was found by fishermen in their nets off the coast of Cape Artemisium in 1928. The figure is more than 2 m in height," http://commons.wikimedia.org/wiki/File%3ANetuno19b.jpg.

Doric Architecture[81]

---

[81] Heinz-Josef Lücking, "An example of the early archaic Doric order- Temple of Poseidon in Paestum, Italy," columns, http://commons.wikimedia.org/wiki/File%3ADoric_order_-_Temple_of_Poseidon_-_Paestum_-_Italy.JPG, Antony McCallum, "Northington Grange England - Europe's first house designed with all external detail of a Greek temple," architecture, http://commons.wikimedia.org/wiki/File%3ANorthingtonGrangeFullFront.jpg.

Corinthian Architecture[82]

---

[82] Wetman, "Architects' first real look at the Greek Ionic order: Julien David LeRoy, *Les ruines plus beaux des monuments de la Grèce* Paris, 1758 (Plate XX)," 18th century copperplate engraving, http://commons.wikimedia.org/wiki/File: SixIonicOrders.jpg, "Midtbygningen, Universitetet i Oslo (Karl Johan)," architecture, http://commons.wikimedia.org/ wiki/File%3AUniversitetet_i_Oslo%2C_midtbygningen3.jpg, and ChrisO, "Maison Carrée, Nîmes, France, 14 BC," architecture, http://commons.wikimedia.org/wiki/File: Maison_ carree_side.jpg.

Hellenistic (c.300s-100s)[83]

---

[83] "Aphrodite of Milos (Venus de Milo) at the Louvre," statue, http://commons.wikimedia.org/wiki/File%3A Aphrodite_ of_Milos.jpg. LivioAndronico, "Laocoön and his sons, also known as the Laocoön Group. Marble, copy after an Hellenistic original from ca. 200 BC. Found in the Baths of Trajan, 1506," http://commons.wikimedia.org/wiki/File%3A Laocoon_and_His_Sons.jpg, "Apollo of the Belvedere," Roman marble copy of, possibly a Greek version dating to the 4th century, http://commons.wikimedia.org/wiki/File%3A Apollo_of_the_Belvedere.jpg.

Quiz 5 for Chapter 5

1-2. According to the Latin poet Virgil, how did the Romans consider themselves in relationship to the Greeks? Also, according to the Virgil, how did the Romans regard the Greeks?

    1.

    2.

3. Contrast, as explained by Apostolos N. Athanassakis, Hesiod's Greek understanding of the world's origin with the Genesis account.

4-14. Match the following: Aphrodite, Chaos, Cyclopes, Eros, Gaia, Cronos, Uranus, Pontus, Zeus, Prometheus, and Tartaros:

| 4. | Existed before the Gods and had a beginning |
| 5. | The Abyss |

6.	The Sea
7.	Love
8.	Mother Earth
9.	Goddess of Love born out of sea foam.
10.	Son of Rhea. He overthrows his father.
11.	The Heavens
12.	Leader of the Titans and son of Mother Earth
13.	One-Eyed Giants
14.	Gave fire to men.

15-18. With respect to flood myths and other stories that are similar to passages in Genesis, explain the Augustinian concept of an original revelation.

19-29. Match the following: Homer, Dionysius, Sophocles, Sappho, Achilles, Odysseus, Helen, Hesiod, Paris, Aristophanes.

19.	*Iliad*
20.	Main hero of the *Iliad*
21.	*Odyssey*

Chapter 5: Greek Culture

22.	*Theogony*
23.	Married to King Menelaus
24.	The Trojan who stole King Menelaus's wife
25.	Woman Greek Lyric Poet
26.	Hero of the *Odyssey*
27.	Greek Playwright of Comedies
28.	God of wine and fertility
29.	Greek Playwright of Tragedies

30-31. Name the two causes of the Trojan War as described by Greek myths.

30.

31.

32. Match the following: Aristotle, Plato, Thales, Democritus, Socrates, Heraclitus, Sophists, and Parmenides.

32.	He thought water is the most basic element.
33.	He thought atoms are the most fundamental

		particles of the cosmos.
	34.	This school taught how to argue regardless of the position held.
	35.	He held that only oneness is real while change is an illusion.
	36.	He held that only change is ultimately real.
	37.	Against the Sophists, he defended the existence of justice and other virtues.
	38.	Teacher of Aristotle
	39.	Teacher of Alexander the Great

40-41. How is the Hippocratic Oath in accordance with natural law that is upheld by Catholic moral teaching?

Chapter 6

Roman Civilization

Introduction

In this chapter and the following chapter, we will study the Romans, the third civilization that, along with the Jewish and Greek civilizations, contributed foundational features to Western Civilization. The Romans began as one of many Italian city-states. Similar to how Alexander the Great and his father united the Greek city-states, the Romans united the many foci of Italian power under their authority. They did so by relying on their military, their sense of law, and their various system of governance, namely Republicanism and Monarchy.

Roman Origins

Similar to Greek history, Italy was once divided into many city-states, of which Rome was but one situated in the region of Latium. The formation of Rome began in the middle of the seventh century BC.[84] According to legend,

---

[84] Francesca Fulminante, *The Urbanisation of Rome and*

Rome was founded in 753 BC by Romulus after he killed his brother Remus and named the city he ruled after himself. *Latium Vetus* (*Latium* of the old) was located in the middle of Italian lands alongside the western coast. The Tiber River runs through *Latium,* giving its inhabitants ease of access to the coast and sea.[85]

The *Latium* city of Rome naturally developed by fertile land that borders the Tiber River.

The hills by the Tiber River, formed by volcanic activity, were also ideal for the Romans since they allowed the Romans to easily defend their cities. A natural land bridge, in the form of an island, also was used by the Romans to swiftly move from one side of the Tiber River to the other.[86] Up until the fourth century BC, the Romans honed their military skills by defending their fertile lands from repeated raids by their envious neighbors.[87] The modern version of the *Latium* region is called in Italian *Lazio,* one of the twenty regions of Italy.

Latium Vetus: From the Bronze Age to the Archaic Era (New York: Cambridge University Press, 2014), 1.

[85] Ibid., 36.
[86] Ibid., 39–40.
[87] Ibid.

Maps of *Latium Vetus* and Modern Day *Lazio*[88]

---

[88] *The Historical Atlas* by William R. Shepherd, 1911, "Early Latium and Campania," map, https://commons.wikimedia.org/wiki/File%3ALatium_et_Campania.png, and "Lazio in Italy," map, https://it.wikipedia.org/wiki/File:Lazio_ in_Italy.svg.

Roman Military

The desire to defend their valuable, ideally located land motivated the Romans to form a military culture. The man who is traditionally attributed to giving Roman culture a distinctly military character is Rome's sixth Estruscan king, Servius Tullius (c. 578-534 BC). A Roman constitution, called the Servian constitution, is attributed to him. This constitution mandated a census in order to determine how many male Roman citizens there were so as to tax them and to require military service from them. The Roman historian Livy (c. 59 BC – 17 AD) in his *History of Rome* credited Servius with consolidating power, establishing a census, organizing the male citizens according to military rank, and encouraging worship of the Goddess Diana, Goddess of Hunting. In Greek her name is Artemis:

> [1.42] Servius consolidated his power quite as much by his private as by his public measures. ... Then he set himself to by far the greatest of all works in times of peace. Just as Numa had been the author of religious laws and institutions, so posterity extols Servius as the founder of those divisions and classes in the State by which a clear distinction is drawn between the various grades of dignity and fortune. He instituted the census, a most beneficial institution in what was to be a great empire, in order that by its means the various duties of peace and

war might be assigned, not as heretofore, indiscriminately, but in proportion to the amount of property each man possessed. From it he drew up the classes and centuries and the following distribution of them, adapted for either peace or war.

[1.43] Those whose property amounted to, or exceeded 100,000 lbs. weight of copper were formed into eighty centuries, forty of juniors and forty of seniors. These were called the First Class. The seniors were to defend the City, the juniors to serve in the field. The armor which they were to provide themselves with comprised helmet, round shield, greaves, and coat of mail, all of brass; these were to protect the person. Their offensive weapons were spear and sword. To this class were joined two centuries of carpenters whose duty it was to work the engines of war; they were without arms. The Second Class consisted of those whose property amounted to between 75,000 and 100,000 lbs. weight of copper; they were formed, seniors and juniors together, into twenty centuries. Their regulation arms were the same as those of the First Class, except that they had an oblong wooden shield instead of the round brazen one and no coat of mail. The Third Class he formed of those whose property fell as low as 50,000 lbs.; these also consisted of twenty centuries, similarly divided into seniors and juniors. The only difference in the armor was that they did not wear greaves. In the Fourth Class were those whose property did not fall below 25,000 lbs. They also formed twenty centuries; their only arms were a spear and a javelin. The Fifth Class was larger it formed thirty centuries. They carried slings and stones, and they included the supernumeraries, the horn-blowers, and the trumpeters, who formed three centuries. This Fifth Class was assessed at 11,000 lbs. The rest of the population whose property fell below this were formed into one century and were exempt from military service.

...

[1.45] After the State was augmented by the expansion of the City and all domestic arrangements adapted to the requirements of both peace and war, Servius endeavored to extend his dominion by state-craft, instead of aggrandizing it by arms, and at the same time made an addition to the adornment of the City. The temple of the Ephesian Diana was famous at that time, and it was reported to have been built by the co-operation of the states of Asia. Servius had been careful to form ties of hospitality and friendship with the chiefs of the Latin nation, and he used to speak in the highest praise of that co-operation and the common recognition of the same deity. By constantly dwelling on this theme he at length induced the Latin tribes to join with the people of Rome

Chapter 6: Roman Civilization

in building a temple to Diana in Rome.[89]

The Romans developed a system of rewards and harsh punishments, called decimation, in order to further motivate its men to fight. The Greek historian Polybius (c. 200-118 BC) in his history on Rome records this Roman carrot and stick methodology:

> If it happens that many are at one time guilty of the same fault, and that whole companies retire before the enemy, and desert their station; instead of punishing all of them by death, an expedient is employed which is both useful and full of terror. The tribune, assembling together all the soldiers of the legion, commands the criminals to be brought forward: and, having sharply reproached them with their cowardice, he then draws out by lot either five, or eight, or twenty men, according to the number of those that have offended. For the proportion is usually so adjusted, that every tenth man is reserved for punishment. Those, who are thus separated from the rest by lot, are bastinadoed without remission in the manner before described. The others are sentenced to be fed with barley instead of wheat; and are lodged without the entrench-

---

[89] Livy, Livy's History of Rome, Vol. 1, trans. Canon Roberts (London: J.M. Dent & Sons, Ltd, 1905), http://mcadams.posc.mu.edu/txt/ah/Livy/Livy01.html

ment, exposed to insults from the enemy. As the danger, therefore, and the dread of death, hangs equally over all the guilty, because no one can foresee upon whom the lot will fall; and as the shame and infamy of receiving barley only for their support is extended also alike to all; this institution is perfectly well contrived, both for impressing present terror, and for the prevention of future faults.

The method by which the young men are animated to brave all danger is also admirable. When an action has passed in which any of the soldiers have shown signal proofs of courage, the consul, assembling the troops together, commands those to approach who have distinguished themselves by any eminent exploit. And having first bestowed on every one of them apart the commendation that is due to this particular instance of their valor and recounted likewise all their former actions that have ever merited applause, he then distributes among them the following rewards. To him who has wounded an enemy, a javelin. To him who has killed an enemy, and stripped him of his armor, if he be a soldier in the infantry, a goblet; if in the cavalry, furniture for his horse; though, in former times, this last was presented only with a javelin. These rewards, however, are not bestowed upon the soldiers who, in a general battle, or in the attack of a city, wound or spoil an enemy; but upon those alone who, in separate skirmishes, and when any occasion offers, in which no necessity requires them to engage in single contest, throw themselves voluntarily into danger, and with design provoke the combat. When a city is taken by storm, those who mount first upon the walls are honored with a golden crown. Those also who have saved the lives of any of the citizens, or the allies, by covering them from the enemy in the time of battle, receive presents from the consul, and are crowned likewise by the persons themselves who have thus been preserved, and who, if they refuse this office, are compelled by the judgment of the tribunes to perform it.[90]

Roman Law

The Western value of law is not only due to Jewish and Greek civilization, as discussed in previous chapters, but also in great part to Roman law and order that logically flowed from their military culture. The Romans first wrote down their laws around 450 BC after the common people demanded a written code of law in order ensure justice.

---

[90] Polybius, *History: Rome at the End of the Punic Wars Constitution of the Roman Republic*, bk., 6, trans. Oliver J. Thatcher, Internet Ancient History Sourcebook, http://www.constitution.org/rom/polybius6.htm

These laws are known as the Twelve Tablets. In the following century (300s BC) a Roman official called a *praetor* was elected by Rome's citizens with the expectation that he would administer justice according to the written laws of the Twelve Tablets. In the subsequent century (200s BC) an official was place in charge of settling disputes between Roman citizens and non-Roman citizens. This precipitated the development of two types of laws, one for the citizens called *jus civile* and one for non-citizens called *jus gentium*.[91]

When Rome replaced its republic with an empire under its first emperor Caesar Augustus (reigned 27 BC – 14 AD), its approach to law once again developed. During this phase the distinction between *jus civile* and *jus gentium* lessened until finally under Emperor Caracalla in 212 AD it was reduced drastically when he offered Roman citizenship to all free people living in his empire. A distinction was made, though, between citizens of higher rank and citizens of lower rank. Nonetheless, a sense of one rule of law applicable to all was present.[92]

When Christianity was allowed to freely practice in 313 AD by the Edict of Milan, Roman law was adopted by Christian rulers. One particularly notable example is Emperor Justinian (reigned 527-565) who ordered Roman

---

[91] Gavin Lewis, *WCIV*, Volume 1: To 1700, Instructor Edition (Boston: Wadsworth, 2012), 92, 110-111.

[92] Ibid., 121.

Chapter 6: Roman Civilization

law and Roman jurisprudence in various works: *Codex Justinianus*, the *Pandects*, and the *Digestum*.[93] These works are foundational to Western Civilization's understanding of law.

Part of the philosophical underpinnings of these Roman Laws is the idea of a natural law traceable to the Roman philosophical school of Stoicism. According to the Stoics, as pithily stated by Cicero, "man is born for justice, and that law and equity are not a mere establishment of opinion, but an institution of nature."[94] Cicero grounded the unchanging aspect of law in God. He asserts that "the entire universe is overruled by the power of God, that by his nature, reason, energy, mind and divinity, or some other word of clearer signification, all things are governed and directed...."[95] Even

---

[93] "Corpus Iuris Civilis," CUA, http://faculty.cua.edu/pennington/Law508/Roman%20Law/Justinian.html; "Medieval Sourcebook: Corpus Iuris Civilis, 6th Century," Internet History Sourcebooks Project, http://legacy.fordham.edu/halsall/source/corpus1.asp. The IHSP cites the following. *The Digest of Justinian*, C. H. Monro, ed. (Cambridge, Mass.: Cambridge Unversity Press, 1904).

[94] Marcus Tullius Cicero, "Marcus Tullius Cicero, The Political Works of Marcus Tullius Cicero, vol. 2 (Treatise on the Laws) [-51]," trans. Francis Barham, bk., 1, 45, Online Library of Liberty, http://oll.libertyfund.org/titles/545

[95] Marcus Tullius Cicero, "Marcus Tullius Cicero, The Political Works of Marcus Tullius Cicero, vol. 2 (Treatise on

though he looked up to the Greeks, as Virgil and other Romans did, Cicero held that the Roman understanding of law, grounded in Divine Law, surpasses the Greek concept of law. He explains:

~ Cicero on Greek Law (*nomos*) and Roman Law (*lex*) ~

> They therefore conceive that the voice of conscience is a law, that moral prudence is a law, whose operation is to urge us to good actions, and restrain us from evil ones. They think, too, that the Greek name for law (νομος), which is derived from νεμω, to distribute, implies the very nature of the thing, that is, to give every man his due. For my part, I imagine that the moral essence of law is better expressed by its Latin name, (*lex*), which conveys the idea of selection or discrimination. According to the Greeks, therefore, the name of law implies an equitable distribution of goods: according to the Romans, an equitable discrimination between good and evil.
>
> The true definition of law should, however, include both these characteristics. And this being granted as an almost self-evident proposition, the origin of justice is to be sought in the divine law of eternal and immutable

---

the Laws) [-51]," trans. Francis Barham, bk., 1, 40, Online Library of Liberty, http://oll.libertyfund.org/titles/545

morality. This indeed is the true energy of nature, the very soul and essence of wisdom, the test of virtue and vice. But since every discussion must relate to some subject, whose terms are of frequent occurrence in the popular language of the citizens, we shall be sometimes obliged to use the same terms as the vulgar, and to conform to that common idiom which signifies by the word law, all the arbitrary regulations which are found in our statute books, either commanding or forbidding certain actions.[96]

Another significant way in which Cicero, representing Stoicism, developed Greek thought in a way that has profoundly influenced Western thought is his defense of human equality. He encourages his fellow Romans not, "to forget the fraternal equality of men". That men are fundamentally equal was not held by Greek philosophers, including by Plato and Aristotle.[97]

---

[96] Marcus Tullius Cicero, "Marcus Tullius Cicero, The Political Works of Marcus Tullius Cicero, vol. 2 (Treatise on the Laws) [-51]," trans. Francis Barham, bk., 1, 37-38, Online Library of Liberty, http://oll.libertyfund.org/titles/545

[97] Jean Porter, *Natural and Divine Law: Reclaiming the Tradition for Christian Ethics* (Grand Rapids: Wm. Eerdmans, 1999), 68.

Roman Governance: Republic and Monarchy

Western styled democracy is inspired more from the representational democracy of Roman Republic (509-27 BC) than by the direct democracy of Athens Greece. Unlike a direct democracy, where all citizens directly make laws, judge laws and execute laws, in a representational democracy citizens elect leaders to represent them in making, judging and executing laws. The Greek historian Polybius (c. 200-118 BC) in his history on Rome details how the Roman Republic's system of democratic representation works. Essential to the Roman Republican form of government was a separation of political powers in order to ensure adequate checks and balances.

~ Polybius - The Constitution of the Roman Republic ~

As for the Roman constitution, it had three elements, each of them possessing sovereign powers: ... that no one could say for certain, not even a native, whether the constitution as a whole were an aristocracy or democracy or despotism. And no wonder: for if we confine our observation to the power of the Consuls we should be inclined to regard it as despotic; if on that of the Senate, as aristocratic; and if finally one looks at the power possessed by the people it would seem a clear case of a democracy. What the exact powers of these several parts were, and still, with slight modifications, are, I will now state.

The Consuls, before leading out the legions, remain in Rome and are supreme masters of the administration. All other magistrates, except the Tribunes, are under them and take their orders. They introduce foreign ambassadors to the Senate; bring matters requiring deliberation before it; and see to the execution of its decrees. If, again, there are any matters of state which require the authorization of the people, it is their business to see to them, to summon the popular meetings, to bring the proposals before them, and to carry out the decrees of the majority. …

The Senate has first of all the control of the treasury, and regulates the receipts and disbursements alike. …

After this one would naturally be inclined to ask what part is left for the people in the constitution, when the Senate has these various functions, especially the control of the receipts and expenditure of the exchequer; and when the Consuls, again, have absolute power over the details of military preparation, and an absolute authority in the field? There is, however, a part left the people, and it is a most important one. For the people is the sole fountain of honor and of punishment; and it is by these two things and these alone that dynasties and constitutions and, in a word, human society are held together: for where the distinction between them is not sharply drawn both in theory and practice, there no undertaking can be properly administered,—as indeed we might expect when good and bad are held in exactly the same honor. The people then are the only court to decide matters of life and death; and even in cases where the penalty is money, if the sum to be assessed is sufficiently serious, and especially when the accused have held the higher magistracies. And in regard to this arrangement there is one point deserving especial commendation and record. Men who are on trial for their lives at Rome, while sentence is in process of being voted,—if even only one of the tribes whose votes are needed to ratify the sentence has not voted,—have the privilege at Rome of openly departing and condemning themselves to a voluntary exile. Such men are safe at Naples or Praeneste or at Tibur, and at other towns with which this arrangement has been duly ratified on oath.[98]

---

[98] Polybius, *The Histories of Polybius*, trans. Evelyn Shirley Shuckburgh, Project Gutenberg, "*The Histories of Polybius*" http://www.gutenberg.org/files/44125/44125-h/44125-h.htm Book VI, Section V, 11-14.

In 27 BC, the Roman Republic, with its representational democratic aspects, described above by Polybius, came to a conclusive end when Gaius Octavius (reigned 27 BC-14 AD), grand-nephew of Gaius Julius Caesar (reigned as dictator of the Roman Republic 49-44 BC), established the Roman Empire. When his great-uncle and dictator Julius Caesar was assassinated by group of irate Roman senators led by Marcus Junius Brutus, a civil war broke out. Octavius was a key player in this civil war. He emerged victorious. After sharing his power as military dictator with Mark Antony and Marcus Lepidus, in what is referred to as the Second Triumvirate,[99] Octavius defeated the two other military dictators. He then established the Roman Empire and in time assumed the title *Imperator Caesar Divi Filius Augustus*, Emperor Caesar Augustus Son of God. The true son of God, Jesus Christ, was born under this Emperor's reign known as the *Pax Romana*, the Roman Peace.[100]

During this time of peace, the Roman Empire expanded,

---

[99] The First Triumvirate consisted of Julius Caesar, Crassus, and Pompey. It ended when a civil war erupted among the three.

[100] Matthew Bunson, *A Dictionary of the Roman Empire* (New York: Oxford University Press, 1995), 45-46, 62, 204, 429-430; Adrian Goldsworthy traces the "Son of God" part of Augustus' name to when Julius Caesar was deified in 42 BC. Adrian Goldsworthy, *Augustus: First Emperor of Rome* (New Haven: Yale University Press, 2014), 131.

its networks of roads were improved, and the language, architecture (most notably the Roman arch), law and customs of the Romans spread throughout the vast empire. One very evident legacy of Roman influence are the many modern languages which are rooted in Latin. These languages are called the Romance languages. The five most well-known of these Latin-based languages are Spanish, Portuguese, French, Italian and Romanian.

Quiz 6 for Chapter 6

1. Compare Rome and Italy with Athens and Greece. Include in your answer the following term, city states.

2-3. Explain geographically why the city of Rome was ideally situated. Also, how did this location motivate the Romans to develop a military culture?

Chapter 6: Roman Civilization

4. How did Rome's sixth Etruscan king, Servius Tullius (c. 578-534 BC) give Rome a military character?

5-6. How did the Romans positively and negatively motivate their men to fight? Include in your answer the term decimation.

    5.

    6.

7. Why did the common people around 450 BC insist upon a written code of law that became known as the Twelve Tablets?

8-9. How did Cicero contrast the Greek concept of law with the Roman understanding?

10. As mentioned in the chapter six, what is one major historical source for the Western notion of equality?

11-13. Compare and contrast ancient Athenian democracy with the democracy present in the Roman Republic. Which form of democracy did the Western civilization primarily adopt?

Chapter 7

Roman Culture

Introduction

As we did with Greek civilization, in this chapter we will study the Roman contribution to Western Civilization by looking at various aspects of Roman culture, specifically, religion, literature, and architecture.

Roman Gods

The vast majority of the Roman Gods were adopted from Greek mythology and then renamed. The following chart[101] shows some of the renamed gods and goddesses.

Greek Name	Roman Name	Identification
Helios	Sol	Sun God
Gaia	Tellus	Mother Earth
Cronus	Saturn	Leader of the

---

[101] "Roman vs. Greek," in the *Encyclopedia Mythica*, http://www.pantheon.org/miscellaneous/roman_vs_greek.html.

		Titans
Zeus	Jupiter	Sky God
Hera	Juno	Goddess of Marriage
Hades	Pluto	God of the Dead
Poseidon	Neptune	God of the Sea
Athena	Minerva	Goddess of Wisdom and War
Aphrodite	Venus	Goddess of Love and Beauty
Ares	Mars	God of War
Hermes	Mercury	Messenger of the Gods
Dionysus	Bacchus	God of Wine
Eros	Cupid	God of Love
Eris	Discordia	Goddess of Discord
Zephyrus	Favonius	Wind God
Charites	Gratiae	Three Minor Goddesses
Irene	Pax	Goddess of Peace
Persephone	Proserpina	Goddess of the Dead
Hygieia	Salus	Goddess of Health

The myths about these various Gods are multiple and sometimes contradict one another, but this did not bother the Romans and the Greeks. As the Roman writer Marcus Terentius Varro (116-27 BC) explained, what is important about the myths is not that the gods exist but that the people

Chapter 7: Roman Culture

worship them in order unite their city.[102] For this reason, unlike Christians, the Romans and Greeks did not have a developed sense of heresy. Right civic worship and not right belief, especially since the myths repeatedly contradicted one another, was important for the Romans and Greeks. For this reason, Socrates was condemned by his fellow Athenians for promoting impiety and not for heresy.[103]

The myths the Romans used to unite their cities were not exclusively from the Greeks. Mithra was one important God of non-Greek origins that Romans worshiped. Worship of Mithra stems from the cult of an Indo-Iranian God which dates back to the second century before the birth of Christ.[104] According to a Mithraic inscription at Rome's Santa Prisca Mithraeum, Mithra, "saved us after shedding the eternal blood."[105] The shed blood refers to a myth in which Mithra slaughters a bull. The world, further explains the myth, comes forth from the blood of this bull.[106]

---

[102] Joseph Ratzinger, *Volk und Haus Gottes in Augustins Lehre von der Kirche* (Sankt Ottilien: Eos Verlag, 1992), 267-271; Cf *De civ Dei* VI 5 Sp 180-182.

[103] Phillip Cary, *The History of Christian Theology*, Lectures 1-18 (Chantilly: The Teaching Company, 2008), 96-97.

[104] Payam Nabarz, *The Mysteries of Mithras: The Pagan Belief That Shaped the Christian World* (Rochester: Inner Traditions, 2005), 1.

[105] Nabarz, *The Mysteries of Mithras*, 8

[106] Nabarz, *The Mysteries of Mithras*, 24-25.

The Romans also believed that their sacrificing and creating God Mithra was born on December 25th from a virgin.[107] In addition to this belief, during the second century after the birth of Christ Romans honored Mithras by sacrificing a bull on March 24th. The blood of the bull was then allowed to run over a person situated beneath the altar. After this ritual, the person was considered "reborn for eternity."[108] With respect to the similarity of important liturgical calendar dates in Mithraism and in Christianity, Pope Benedict XVI, prior to his election to the papacy, explained:

> The claim used to be made that December 25 developed in opposition to the Mithras myth, or as a Christian response to the cult of the unconquered sun promoted by Roman emperors in the third century in their efforts to establish a new imperial religion. However, these old theories can no longer be sustained. The decisive factor was the connection of creation and Cross, of creation and Christ's conception. In the light of the "hour of Jesus", these dates brought the cosmos into the picture. The cosmos was now thought of as the pre-annunciation of Christ, the Firstborn of creation (cf. Col 1:15). It is he of

---

[107] Nabarz, *The Mysteries of Mithras*, 4, 19, 48.

[108] Henry M. Sayre, *The Humanities: Culture, Continuity & Change*, Book 2 (Upper Saddle River: Prentice Hall, 2012), 261-262.

whom creation speaks, and it is by him that its mute message is deciphered. The cosmos finds its true meaning in the Firstborn of creation, who has now entered history. From him comes the assurance that the adventure of creation, of a world with its own free existence distinct from God, does not end up in absurdity and tragedy but, throughout all its calamities and upheavals, remains something positive. God's blessing of the seventh day is truly and definitively confirmed.[109]

As Pope Benedict points out, Christians dated Christ's birth on December 25 not out of competition with Mithraism but rather in accordance with an ancient tradition that held that the Creation of the world, Christ's conception, and Christ's Passion occurred on the same day of the year, March 25th.[110] Nine months later, about the typical time a woman is pregnant, Christ was born on December 25th:

> Let us turn albeit briefly to the second focal point of the Church's year, the Christmas season, which developed somewhat later than the cycle that leads to and comes from Easter. ... It is hard to say how far back the beginnings of the Christmas feast go. It assumed its defi-

---

[109] Joseph Ratzinger, *The Spirit of the Liturgy*, trans. John Saward (San Francisco: Ignatius Press, 2000), 105-108.

[110] Ratzinger, *The Spirit of the Liturgy*, 105-107.

nitive form in the third century.

At about the same time the feast of the Epiphany emerged in the East on January 6 and the feast of Christmas in the West on December 25. The two feasts had different emphases because of the different religious and cultural contexts in which they arose, but essentially their meaning was the same: the celebration of the birth of Christ as the dawning of the new light, the true sun, of history. ... Astonishingly, the starting point for dating the birth of Christ was March 25.

As far as I know, the most ancient reference to it is in the writings of the African ecclesiastical author Tertullian (c. 150-c. 207), who evidently assumes as well-known tradition that Christ suffered death on March 25. In Gaul, right up to the sixth century, this was kept as the immovable date of Easter. In a work on the calculation of the date of Easter, written in A.D. 243, and also emanating from Africa, we find March 25 interpreted as the day of the world's creation, and, in connection with that, we find a very peculiar dating for the birth of Christ.

According to the account of creation in Genesis 1, the sun was created on the fourth day, that is, on March 28. This day should, therefore, be regarded as the day of Christ's birth, as the rising of the true sun of history. This idea was altered during the third century, so that the day of Christ's Passion and the day of his conception were regarded as identical. On March 25 the Church honored both the Annunciation by the angel and the Lord's conception by the Holy Spirit in the womb of the Virgin. The feast of Christ's birth on December 25 - nine months after March 25 - developed in the West in the course of the third century, while the East - probably because of a difference of calendar - at first celebrated January 6 as the birthday of Christ. It may also have been the response to a feast of the birth of the mythical gods observed on this day in Alexandria.[111]

Roman Literature

Some of the most notable of ancient Roman writers are Cicero (106-43 BC), Catullus (84-54 BC), Virgil (70-19 BC), Horace (65-8 BC), and Ovid (43 BC-17 AD). With respect to law, we have already looked at Cicero's Stoic development of Greek philosophy. He also wrote, from a Roman perspective, on many other aspects of Greek culture. Catullus, Virgil, Horace, and Ovid are significant poets who greatly influenced Western civilization with their prose. A few of their most important works include the following.

Horace's famous collection of poetry is called the *Odes*. Ovid's *Metamorphoses* is one of the major sources for Roman mythology. Virgil's epic poem the *Aeneid* tells the

---

[111] Joseph Ratzinger, *The Spirit of the Liturgy*, trans. John Saward (San Francisco: Ignatius Press, 2000), 105-108.

tale of the Trojan hero Aeneas who, after the Trojan War, goes to Italy where he becomes a father of the Roman people. Note that the Romans looked up to the Trojan Aeneas who only plays a small role in Homer's *Illiad*. This is in contrast with the Greeks who saw the Greek hero Achilles as the hero of the Trojan War.

~ Virgil in his *Aeneid* Describing Aeneas's Destiny ~

Arms and the man [Aeneid] I sing, who first made way, predestined exile, from the Trojan shore to Italy, the blest Lavinian strand. Smitten of storms he was on land and sea by violence of Heaven, to satisfy stern Juno's sleepless wrath; and much in war he suffered, seeking at the last to found the city, and bring o'er his fathers' gods to safe abode in Latium; whence arose the Latin race, old Alba's reverend lords, and from her hills wide-walled, imperial Rome.[112]

---

[112] Virgil "Aeneid," Perseus Digital Library, http://www.perseus.tufts.edu/hopper/text?doc=Perseus%3Atext%3A1999.02.0054%3Abook%3D1%3Acard%3D1. The following source is cited. Vergil, *Aeneid*, trans. Theodore C. Williams, (Boston: Houghton Mifflin Co., 1910).

~ Horace *Do not Ask* Poem ~

Ask not ('tis forbidden knowledge), what our destined term of years, Mine and yours; nor scan the tables of your Babylonish seers.

Better far to bear the future, my Leuconoe, like the past, Whether Jove has many winters yet to give, or this our last;

This, that makes the Tyrrhene billows spend their strength against the shore. Strain your wine and prove your wisdom; life is short; should hope be more? In the moment of our talking, envious time has ebb'd away.

Seize the present; trust tomorrow e'en as little as you may.[113]

~ Catullus on Love ~

I hate and I love. Why I do this, perhaps you ask. I know not, but I feel it happening and I am tortured.[114]

---

[113] Horace, "Q. Horatius Flaccus (Horace), *Odes*, John Conington, Ed.," Od. 1.11, Perseus, http://www.perseus.tufts.edu/hopper/text?doc=Perseus%3Atext%3A1999.02.0025%3Abook%3D1%3Apoem%3D1 1

[114] Catullus, "C. Valerius Catullus, *Carmina*, Leonard C. Smithers, Ed." No. 85, Perseus, http://www.perseus.tufts.edu/

Roman Architecture

In adopting Greek architecture, and architecture from other cultures, Romans developed certain features, most notably the arch. To span space, Greek architects relied primarily on the simple post and lintel technique in which a horizontal beam spans two vertical columns. The Romans, in contrast, relied extensively on the use of an arch to span space between columns. This allowed their buildings to have fewer columns and more interior space.

Examples of Roman arches are below. The last example is an aqueduct which the Romans, relying upon gravity, used to transport water over extensive distances. After drilling through mountains, they also used siphons to keep their "artificial rivers"[115] flowing. While not the first to employ aqueducts, the Romans were the first to use them in an extensive, systematic manner. Surprisingly, the main function of the aqueducts was not to provide households with water, since Romans relied upon wells and cisterns for household needs, but instead to supply water for Roman baths, a luxury Romans enjoyed. In addition to this primary purpose, the water from these man-made rivers flowed into

---

hopper/text?doc=Perseus%3Atext%3A1999.02.0006%3Apoem%3D85.

[115] A. Trevor Hodge, *Roman Aqueducts & Water Supply*, second ed., (London: Bristol Classical Press, 2002), 2, 5-6.

Chapter 7: Roman Culture 143

mills, fountains, toilets, and gardens. The water was also used for shows, and for domestic reasons.[116]

A Typical Arch Design (1st cent. AD)[117]

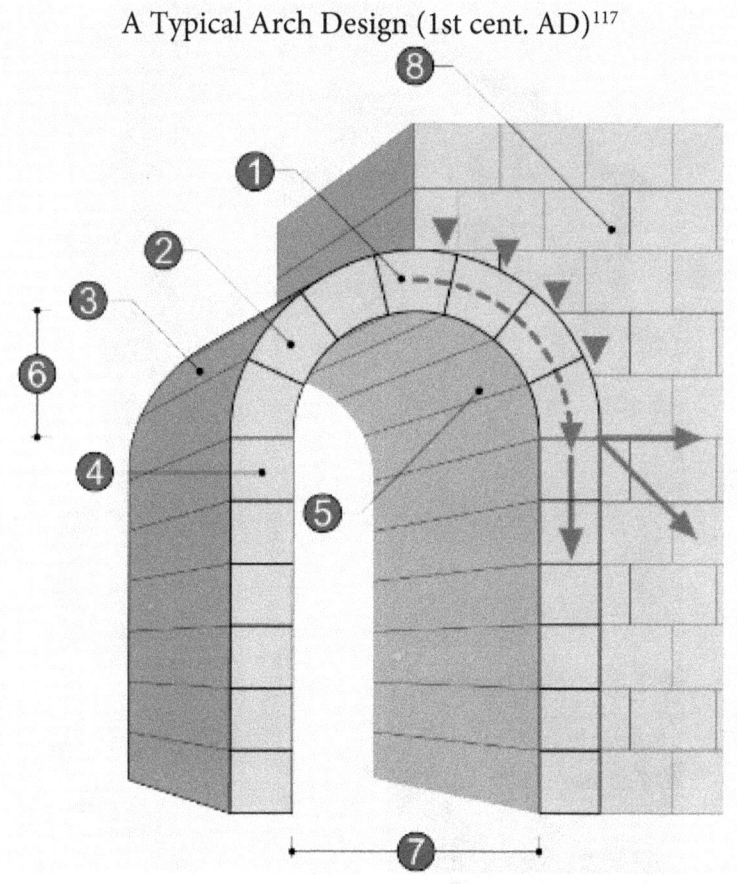

---

[116] A. Trevor Hodge, *Roman Aqueducts & Water Supply*, second ed., (London: Bristol Classical Press, 2002), 2, 5-6.

[117] MesserWoland, "Schematic illustration of an arch," illustration, http://commons.wikimedia.org/wiki/File:Arch_illustration.svg 1. Keystone, 2. Voussoir, 3. Back, 4. Impost, 5. Intrados, 6. Rise, 7. Clear span, "Bay", 8. Abutment

Arch of Titus, Forum Romanum, Rome, Italy (81 AD)[118]

---

[118] Dnalor 01, "Rom, Titusbogen," architecture, http://commons.wikimedia.org/wiki/File%3ARom%2C_Titusbogen_2.jpg

Chapter 7: Roman Culture 145

Arch of Titus, Forum Romanum, Rome, Italy (81 AD)[119]

---

[119] One of the reliefs on this depicts the 70 AD Roman destruction of Jerusalem by Emperor Titus (reigned 79-81 AD). Rabax63 (Diskussion), "Titusbogen Frontansicht (Eingang zum Forum Romanum)," architecture, http://commons.wikimedia.org/wiki/File%3ATitusbogenFront.jpg.

Coliseum of Rome (80 AD)[120]

---

[120] "Roma, Colosseo," architecture, http://commons.wikimedia.org/wiki/File%3ARoma06(js).jpg.

Chapter 7: Roman Culture   147

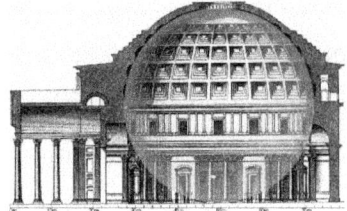

Pantheon (c. 126 AD)[121]

Roman Aqueduct[122]

---

[121] In Greek, Pantheon means all the gods. The Romans built the Pantheon to honor all their gods. The building is now a Catholic Church, St. Mary and the Martyrs. "The interior of the Pantheon (Roma), Giovanni Paolo Panini 1692–1765,) http://commons.wikimedia.org/wiki/File%3A Pantheon-panini.jpg with "Cross-section of the Pantheon in Rome showing how a 43.3 m-diameter sphere fits under its dome," http://commons.wikimedia.org/wiki/File%3APantheon_section_sphere.svg

[122] "Pont du Gard, Roman Empire," architecture, http://commons.wikimedia.org/wiki/File%3APont_du_Gard_Oct_2007.jpg

Another Roman structure that was throughout the empire and which still influences Western architecture is the Roman basilica. For the Romans, a basilica was not a place of worship but instead just a large public hall complete with a central nave, side aisles, and a semicircle space, called an apse, situated at the end of the nave.

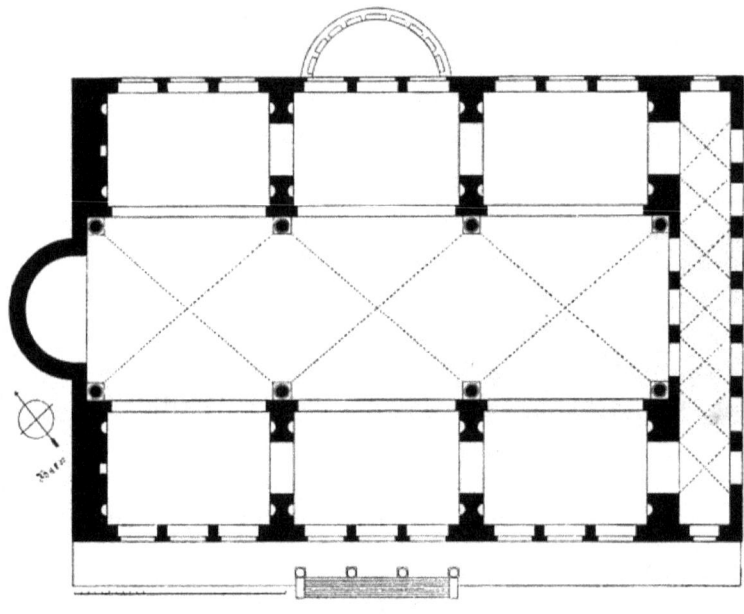

2. ROM: CONSTANTINSBASILICA.

Diagram of a Roman Basilica (312 AD)[123]

---

[123] "Floor plan of the Basilica of Maxentius and Constantine," floorplan, http://commons.wikimedia.org/wiki/File:Dehio_6_Basilica_of_Maxentius_Floor_plan.jpg.

Chapter 7: Roman Culture 149

Remains of a Roman Basilica[124]

---

[124] "Remains of the Basilica of Maxentius and Constantine," The building's northern aisle is all that remains," http://commons.wikimedia.org/wiki/File%3ABasilica_of_Maxentius.JPG.

Quiz 7 for Chapter 7

1-15. Write three short paragraphs on three of the following Gods and/or Goddesses:

Greek Name	Roman Name
Helios	Sol
Gaia	Tellus
Cronus	Saturn
Zeus	Jupiter
Hera	Juno
Hades	Pluto
Poseidon	Neptune
Athena	Minerva
Aphrodite	Venus
Ares	Mars
Hermes	Mercury
Dionysus	Bacchus
Eros	Cupid
Eris	Discordia
Zephyrus	Favonius
Charites	Gratiae
Irene	Pax
Persephone	Proserpina

16-20. Explain why Socrates was condemned by his fellow Athenians. Include reference to Varro in your answer along with myths, gods, and cities.

21-24. Compare and contrast Mithraic belief and practice with Christian belief and practice. Include the following in your answer: baptism, sacrifice, and creation.

25-28. As explained by Benedict XVI, why did early Christians choose December 25th as the day to celebrate Jesus' birthday? Include three reasons in your answer.

Identify the following.

29. Author_____

30. Name of the work _____

> Arms and the man [Aeneas] I sing, who first made way, predestined exile, from the Trojan shore to Italy, the blest Lavinian strand. Smitten of storms he was on land and sea by violence of Heaven, to satisfy stern Juno's sleepless wrath; and much in war he suffered, seeking at the last to found the city, and bring o'er his fathers' gods to safe abode in Latium; whence arose the Latin race, old Alba's reverend lords, and from her hills wide-walled, imperial Rome.[125]

---

[125] Virgil "Aeneid," Perseus Digital Library,

Chapter 7: Roman Culture

31. Author _____

Ask not ('tis forbidden knowledge), what our destined term of years, Mine and yours; nor scan the tables of your Babylonish seers. Better far to bear the future, my Leuconoe, like the past, Whether Jove has many winters yet to give, or this our last; This, that makes the Tyrrhene billows spend their strength against the shore. Strain your wine and prove your wisdom; life is short; should hope be more? In the moment of our talking, envious time has ebb'd away. Seize the present; trust tomorrow e'en as little as you may.[126]

31. Author _____

I hate and I love. Why I do this, perhaps you ask. I know not, but I feel it happening and I am

---

http://www.perseus.tufts.edu/hopper/text?doc=Perseus%3Atext%3A1999.02.0054%3Abook%3D1%3Acard%3D1 The following source is cited. Vergil, *Aeneid*, trans. Theodore C. Williams, (Boston: Houghton Mifflin Co., 1910).

[126] Horace, "Q. Horatius Flaccus (Horace), *Odes*, John Conington, Ed.," Od. 1.11, Perseus, http://www.perseus.tufts.edu/hopper/text?doc=Perseus%3Atext%3A1999.02.0025%3Abook%3D1%3Apoem%3D1 1

tortured.[127]

33-34. According to A. Trevor Hodge's research, what was the primary reason for Roman aqueducts? How is this primary reason similar to the flow of electricity to modern machines, such as the washing machine or air conditioners, which many use regularly?

35. What was the original function of Roman basilicas?

---

[127] Catullus, "C. Valerius Catullus, *Carmina*, Leonard C. Smithers, Ed." No. 85, Perseus, http://www.perseus.tufts.edu/hopper/text?doc=Perseus%3Atext%3A1999.02.0006%3Apoem%3D85

Chapter 8

Early Christian Civilization

Introduction

In the previous chapters, we studied three civilizations: Jewish, Greek, and Roman. Aspects from these civilizations were taken up and transformed by Christianity. The central city that is to inform all desires, thoughts, words, and actions of Christian civilization (from the Latin *civis* meaning city dweller) is the heavenly city of Jerusalem. "Then I saw a new heaven and a new earth; for the first heaven and the first earth had passed away, and the sea was no more. And I saw the holy city, the New Jerusalem, coming down out of heaven from God, prepared as a bride adorned for her husband." (Revelation 21:1-2 NRSV). Christianity carefully discerned which aspects from civilizations that preceded it were to be assimilated and transformed by Christian faith and life. We will study a few ways by which Christians built upon and deepened previous cultures while establishing their own.

Judaism and Christianity

One non-biblical source we have of Christianity in its

earliest stages is from the Roman-Jewish historian Titus Flavius Josephus (37-c.100 AD). The New Testament is, of course, our principal source of Christianity in its earliest stages. We will, therefore, carefully look at the New Testament to know Jesus better and to dismiss misperceptions of Jesus. You will see that some of the features of Jesus' life were in harmony with the Judaism of his time while others were in tension with the dominant form of Judaism of his day. Those aspects of Judaism that were in harmony with the way of life that Jesus proposed to his followers were further developed in Christianity.

Christianity in Jewish History

Josephus wrote number of works including the *Jewish War* (written between 75-79 AD) and the *Jewish Antiquities* (written between 92-94 AD). In his writings, Josephus refers to John the Baptist, Jesus, and James. He also describes the differences between the three main expressions of Judaism at the time of Jesus (Essenes, Pharisees, and Sadducees), the fall of Jerusalem, and the destruction of the Temple by the Romans in 70 AD.[128] Below are two excerpts from Josephus's *Jewish Antiquities*. The first refers John the Baptist, and the

---

[128] Louis Harry Feldman, and Gōhei Hata, *Josephus, Judaism, and Christianity* (Detroit: Wayne State University Press, 1987), 16.

second is on Jesus.

~ Josephus on John the Baptist ~

Now some of the Jews thought that the destruction of Herod's army came from God, and that very justly, as a punishment of what he did against John, that was called the Baptist: for Herod slew him, who was a good man, and commanded the Jews to exercise virtue, both as to righteousness towards one another, and piety towards God, and so to come to baptism; for that the washing [with water] would be acceptable to him, if they made use of it, not in order to the putting away [or the remission] of some sins [only], but for the purification of the body; supposing still that the soul was thoroughly purified beforehand by righteousness. Now when [many] others came in crowds about him, for they were very greatly moved [or pleased] by hearing his words, Herod, who feared lest the great influence John had over the people might put it into his power and inclination to raise a rebellion, [for they seemed ready to do anything he should advise,] thought it best, by putting him to death, to prevent any mischief he might cause, and not bring himself into difficulties, by sparing a man who might make him repent of it when it would be too late. Accordingly he was sent a prisoner, out of Herod's suspicious temper, to Macherus, the castle I before mentioned, and was there put to death. Now the Jews had an opinion that the destruction of this army was sent as a punishment upon Herod, and a mark of God's displeasure to him.[129]

~ Josephus on Jesus ~

Many scholars maintain that there is evidence of Christian tampering with the text in which Josephus refers to "Jesus, a wise man". See below. However, there is another text for which there is scholarly consensus that Josephus wrote it. In this text, also from the *Jewish Antiquities* Josephus states,

> "Festus was now dead, and Albinus was but upon the road; so he assembled the Sanhedrin of judges, and brought before them the brother of Jesus, who was called Christ, whose name was James, and some others, [or, some of his companions]; and when he had formed an accusation against them as breakers of the law, he delivered them to be stoned...."[130]

---

[129] Josephus, "Antiquities of the Jews," bk. 18, chap. 5, no. 2, trans. William Whiston, Project Gutenberg, http://www.gutenberg.org/files/2848/2848-h/2848-h.htm#link202HCH0009.

[130] Flavius Josephus, "Jewish Antiquities," bk, 20, ch. 9, 1,

> Now there was about this time Jesus, a wise man, if it be lawful to call him a man; for he was a doer of wonderful works, a teacher of such men as receive the truth with pleasure. He drew over to him both many of the Jews and many of the Gentiles. He was [the] Christ. And when Pilate, at the suggestion of the principal men amongst us, had condemned him to the cross, those that loved him at the first did not forsake him; for he appeared to them alive again the third day; as the divine prophets had foretold these and ten thousand other wonderful things concerning him. And the tribe of Christians, so named from him, are not extinct at this day. [131]

Jesus in History

The name Jesus comes to the English language, through both Latin and Greek, from the Hebrew word *Yehoshua* which means God saves. This Hebrew word is the Hebrew equivalent of the English name Joshua. After Moses died, the Joshua of the Old Testament led the Israelites into the Promised Land.[132] Similarly, but with a difference, the Joshua

---

Sacred Texts, http://www.sacred-texts.com/jud/josephus/ant-20.htm

[131] Josephus, "Antiquities of the Jews," bk. 18, chap. 3, no. 3.

[132] "Jesus," found in the Online Etymology Dictionary,

(Jesus) of the New Testament offers all entry into a heavenly promised land that transcends history and time.

Jesus as the new savior-leader of the Jewish people, and through the Jews of all people, was born during the reign of Emperor Caesar Augustus and the Roman-Jewish client King Herod the Great (Luke 2:1). Since according to our calendar King Herod the Great is recorded to have died in 4 BC, Jesus was not born in 1 AD (*Anno Domini* means in Latin in the year of the Lord); he actually was born around 4 BC. The dating error of Jesus' birth was originally made by the monk and early Christian scholar Dionysius Exiguus (death c. 550 AD). This monk is credited with introducing the *Anno Domini* (Year of the Lord) calendar that has shaped Western Civilization's concept of time.[133]

The town that Jesus was born in is called Bethlehem, meaning in Hebrew "House of bread." This location of this Judean town anticipated Jesus' later role in life as the sacrificial lamb and savior. Bethlehem is about five miles south of Jerusalem. Its proximity to Jerusalem allowed its shepherds to supply lambs to the Temple for sacrifice, above all for the annual Passover meal.[134] Jesus did not stay for long

---

http://etymonline.com/index.php, *Interlinear NIV Hebrew-English Old Testament* (Numbers 14:30).

[133] Benedict XVI, *Jesus of Nazareth: The Infancy Narratives*, trans. Philip J. Whitmore (New York: Image, 2012), 61-62.

[134] "Babylonian Talmud, Book 2, Chapter VII: Tracts

in this town associated with sheep. According to Luke, the reason why Joseph took his pregnant wife Mary to Bethlehem from their home town of Nazareth, situated not in Judea but in Galilee, was to register for a census issued by Emperor Caesar Augustus. He was required to register in Bethlehem since he was a member of the tribe of Judah and house of David. (Luke 2:1-5)

After fulfilling his civic duty and his religious duty of circumcising, naming, and presenting his child in the Temple of Jerusalem, Joseph returned with Mary and Jesus to their Galilean town of Nazareth. (Luke 2:21-39) According to the Gospel of Matthew, before returning to Nazareth, Joseph fled with Mary and Jesus to Egypt in order to escape the wrath of King Herod. Herod had ordered the murder of all boys under the age of two who lived in or around Bethlehem. He did so since he feared that one of these boys may later challenge his rule. (Matthew 2) About four years later, when King Herod died, Joseph finally returned to Nazareth.

In Nazareth, Joseph taught Jesus the trade of a *tekton*. (Matthew 13:55) This Greek word signifies a builder in hard material. As builders and earners of a moderate income of the time, Joseph's and Jesus' status in society was not at the

---

Erubin, Shekalim, Rosh Hashana, trans. Michael L. Rodkinson, (1918)," Sacred Texts, http://www.sacred-texts.com/jud/t02/shk11.htm.

bottom of the social pecking order. This was reserved for beggars, slaves, and day laborers.[135]

Upon embarking on his three years of public ministry, after being baptized by John the Baptist in the Jordan River (Mark 1:9), Jesus set out to complete the role of the prophet Elijah. Elijah promised that he would return to restore the tribes of Israel. As Sirach states "At the appointed time, it is written, you [Elijah] are destined to calm the wrath of God before it breaks out in fury, to turn the hearts of parents to their children, and to restore the tribes of Jacob." (Sirach 48:10 NRSV) In fulfillment of this mission of gathering people and restoring unity, Jesus tells his disciples that "Elijah is indeed coming and will restore all things." (Matthew 17:11 NRSV)

Jesus also identifies the Twelve Apostles with the Twelve Tribes of Israel, by telling Peter, "Truly I tell you, at the renewal of all things, when the Son of Man is seated on the throne of his glory, you who have followed me will also sit on twelve thrones, judging the twelve tribes of Israel." (Matthew 19:28 NRSV)[136] In continuity with and in fulfillment of Elijah's mission, the Twelve Apostles receive

---

[135] John P. Meier, *Jesus the Marginal Jew*, Volume 3 (New York: Random House, 2001), 620.

[136] Also see Micah 2:12; 2:13; 4:9; Isa 11:1-9, 10-16 11:12 and 59:15-21; 60; Jeremiah 31:1; 30:3-9; cf. 33:14-26; 31:31-34; Ezekiel 20:27-44; 34; 37: 15-28; Tobit 13; Bar 4:21-5:9.

the mandate to gather all people into the one Catholic Church of Jesus Christ. This salvific mission continues in the office of the bishops. The Catholic, which in Greek means pertaining to the whole, dimension of the Church expresses Jesus's mission of gathering all together and saving people corporately and sacramentally through the Church and not simply in an individualistic manner.[137]

Some Misconceptions of Jesus

Sometimes, Jesus is erroneously presented as a poor Jewish man from the lowest class who, with few exceptions, chose equally poor people. At other times, he is identified as a political revolutionary who was intent on overthrowing the Romans. As far as Jesus' poverty goes, while it is true that he was not from the upper classes, neither Sacred Scripture nor extra-biblical sources give any indication that He came from an impoverished upbringing. By being trained as a *tekton*, as explained earlier, Jesus and his adoptive father earned a respectable income for their time. The Apostle Peter, whom Jesus chose to lead the twelve, was also accustomed to a decent income. Peter even owned a home and had a family in Capernaum. (Luke 4:38)

As explained by Meier, "It is well to remember that the

---

[137] Meier, *Jesus the Marginal Jew*, Volume 3, 152-153, 162-163.

fishing business on the Sea of Galilee was a lively and prosperous one, at least for those who owned or oversaw the operations. The romantic idea of Jesus' calling only the impoverished to discipleship finds no confirmation in the sons of Zebedee - nor, for that matter, in Peter with his house and family in Capernaum, nor in Levi the toll collector at Capernaum."[138] Jesus even differentiates himself from the poor by saying, after a woman pours expensive ointment over his head, "She has performed a good service for me. For you always have the poor with you, but you will not always have me." (Matthew 26:10-11 NRSV)[139]

In addition, there is no evidence that Jesus ever promoted any specific political policy. Instead, he typically chose to teach indirectly and mysteriously with parables and, as the biblical scholar John P. Meier describes, with "allusive riddle-like speech."[140] While some of Jesus' followers had definite political leanings, when examined closely, even these political leanings were not well-defined. The Apostle Simon the Zealot was called a zealot not because he belonged to an anti-Roman party, but because of his zeal for practicing the Mosaic Law and his desire for other Jews to do so as well. At the time of Jesus, this was how a zealot was defined.

The political term "Zealots" refers to Jews of the First

---

[138] Meier, *Jesus the Marginal Jew*, Volume 3, 214.

[139] Meier, *Jesus the Marginal Jew*, Volume 3, 620.

[140] Meier, *Jesus the Marginal Jew*, Volume 3, 621-624.

Chapter 8: Early Christian Civilization 165

Jewish War (67-68 AD) who banded together to overthrow the Romans. To claim that Simon the Zealot was a political Zealot is anachronistically erroneous.[141] In Acts, even the high priests who collaborated with the Romans are described as filled with zeal (ζήλου). (Acts 5:17) The Elijah-like mission of Jesus and the Apostles was not defined by political revolution but by gathering (or catching like fishermen) people into the Kingdom of God. Even the most politically savvy of Jesus' Apostles, Judas Iscariot, could not have been part of the Jewish terrorist group called the *sicarri*, as some claim. According to historical record, the *sicarri*, whose members carried daggers to assassinate enemies, was formed in the forties and fifties of the first century AD, well after Judas had committed suicide.[142]

A final argument against the view that Jesus emerged out of an angry social political environment intent on overthrowing the Romans is that Jesus grew up in Galilee and not in Judea. During Jesus' life of earth, Galilee was a peaceful semi-autonomous region. For this reason, the Romans did not station their armies in Galilee. When the Jewish, client king of the Romans, Herod the Great, died in 4 BC, his son Herod Antipas ruled over the semi-autonomous region of Galilee as a tetrarch. Evidence of Galilean semi-autonomy from Roman rule is Antipas' practice of minting his own

---

[141] Meier, *Jesus the Marginal Jew*, Volume 3, 205.
[142] Meier, *Jesus the Marginal Jew*, Volume 3, 210.

money, collecting taxes from his citizens, and then paying from the money collected tribute to the Romans. Galilean Jews demonstrated their appreciation for their relative autonomy from Rome by never once revolting against Herod Antipas' rule. In contrast, the Roman Province of Judea, which was directly ruled by the Romans and where Jesus died, was known for its political instability and strife.[143]

Jesus in Tension with Judaism

A number of aspects of Jesus' way of life were considered jarring to many of the Jewish people. As pointed out by John P. Meier, Jesus' followers called Him a rabbi even though there is no evidence that Jesus received any formal training.[144] Unlike other rabbis of his day, Jesus invited his followers to literally follow him on his travels and not simply teach, as a typical rabbi did. In teaching his followers, Jesus puzzled many, and still does, since at times he appears liberal with respect to traditional practices and at other times intensifies the demands of tradition, especially with respect to marriage as indissoluble, to divorce, and to love of neighbor. The reason for Jesus's apparent liberal tendencies coupled with his apparent traditionalist tendencies are, explains Ratzinger, because Jesus wants us "to know the father from

---

[143] Meier, *Jesus the Marginal Jew*, Volume 3, 618-620.
[144] Meier, *Jesus the Marginal Jew*, Volume 3, 621.

the perspective of tradition and to understand tradition from the perspective of the father." The relationship of tradition to the Father's will is "the key to the combination in Jesus of faithfulness to and criticism of tradition, to the juxtaposition of 'liberal' and the pious that is so puzzling to us when we view it from without."[145]

His practice of celibacy, identification of celibacy with absolute dedication to His mission (Matthew 19:12), along with permitting women, some who had been previously possessed by demons, to accompany him on his journeys was even more atypical to his time. Some of these female companions provided Jesus with food and money. Jesus' requirement of those who closely followed him to leave their family (Luke 9:59-62) was also a disruptive requirement for many Jews since Judaism lacks a pronounced appreciation of celibacy and views maintaining family ties, especially with one's parents, as a solemn duty.[146]

A teaching of Jesus that was the most disturbing of all was when He asserted, "Destroy this temple [Jerusalem Temple], and in three days I will raise it up." (John 2:19).[147]

---

[145] Joseph Cardinal Ratzinger, *Principles of Catholic Theology: Building Stones for a Fundamental Theology*, trans. Mary Francis McCarthy (San Francisco: Ignatius Press, 1987), 98.

[146] Meier, *Jesus the Marginal Jew*, Volume 3, 68, 71, 79, 622.

[147] Meier, *Jesus the Marginal Jew*, Volume 3, 501.

Christians believe he fulfilled these words by rising from the dead.

Jewish Elements in Christianity

Many of aspects of Christianity, especially in Catholicism, come providentially from the Jewish people, specifically through the Jewish group known as the Pharisees. One element of Catholicism that is in continuity with a belief of the Pharisees is the practice of oral tradition.

The Pharisees greatly valued oral tradition. According to the Pharisees, God gave Moses a dual Torah, consisting of a written set of laws and an oral set of laws. They also believed, maintains Josephus, in the immortality of the soul, reward or punishment after death, the resurrection of the dead, the existence of angels, human freedom, and divine providence.[148] The rival group to the Pharisees were the Sad-

---

[148] Josephus, "The Wars Of The Jews, Book II, Book 2, Chapter 8, section 14," Early Jewish Writings, http://www.earlyjewishwritings.com/text/josephus/war2.html "But then as to the two other orders at first mentioned, the Pharisees are those who are esteemed most skillful in the exact explication of their laws, and intro-duce the first sect. These ascribe all to fate [or providence], and to God, and yet allow, that to act what is right, or the contrary, is principally in the power of men, although fate does co-operate in every action. They say that all souls are incorrup-tible, but that the souls of

Chapter 8: Early Christian Civilization

ducees. The Sadducees dominated the leadership of the Temple and closely collaborated with the Romans. They rejected many of the Pharisees' beliefs and practices, especially the Pharisees' esteem for popular oral practices and beliefs. For these reasons, the Sadducees were not well liked by

---

good men only are removed into other bodies, - but that the souls of bad men are subject to eternal punishment. But the Sadducees are those that compose the second order, and take away fate entirely, and suppose that God is not concerned in our doing or not doing what is evil; and they say, that to act what is good, or what is evil, is at men's own choice, and that the one or the other belongs so to everyone, that they may act as they please. They also take away the belief of the immortal duration of the soul, and the punishments and rewards in Hades. Moreover, the Pharisees are friendly to one another, and are for the exercise of concord, and regard for the public; but the behavior of the Sadducees one towards another is in some degree wild, and their conversation with those that are of their own party is as barbarous as if they were strangers to them. And this is what I had to say concerning the philosophic sects among the Jews."; NASB Acts 23: 6-8. "But perceiving that one group were Sadducees and the other Pharisees, Paul [began] crying out in the Council, "Brethren, I am a Pharisee, a son of Pharisees; I am on trial for the hope and resurrection of the dead!" As he said this, there occurred a dissension between the Pharisees and Sadducees, and the assembly was divided. 8For the Sadducees say that there is no resurrection, nor an angel, nor a spirit, but the Pharisees acknowledge them all."

many Jews whereas the Pharisees were.[149]

Hellenism and Christianity

While Judaism provided Christianity with its soul, or heart, the Greeks and their Hellenic culture providentially gave to Christianity an intellectual apparatus to translate the Jewish particularity and intimate sense of being personally called and chosen into more universal terms. However, as Ratzinger reminds us, the personal and particular that Judaism bears within as essential also has primacy in Christianity. Christians believe that the personal is of greater value than universal Greek-like concepts since Christ as the Word of the Father spoken in the Love of the Holy Spirit is a person. All universal concepts find their deepest meaning in the person of Jesus.[150]

Greek elements in Christianity/Catholicism

The Greek influence in the time of Jesus is apparent right in the names of some of the apostles and a name for Jesus. Christ (Χριστός) is the Greek word for the anointed since

---

[149] Meier, *Jesus the Marginal Jew*, Volume 3, 289-388, especially 330-331, 394-396, 400.

[150] Joseph Cardinal Ratzinger, *Introduction to Christianity*, trans. J.R. Foster (San Francisco: Ignatius Press, 1990), 111.

Jesus as the Messiah (מָשִׁיחַ), a Hebrew term, is the anointed one of God. Two of Jesus' Apostles also were referred to with Greek names, specifically Philip (*philo* + *hippos* meaning lover of horses, Andrew (*andreios* meaning manly).[151] According to the Gospel of John, Greeks naturally approached Philip and Andrew. "Now among those who went up to worship at the festival were some Greeks. They came to Philip, who was from Bethsaida in Galilee, and said to him, 'Sir, we wish to see Jesus.' Philip went and told Andrew; then Andrew and Philip went and told Jesus." (John 12:20-21 NRSV)

Even though early followers of Jesus were on friendly terms with some Greeks, and St. Paul actively evangelized them, some Christians wished to completely reject the Greek way of life. One example is the Christian Tertullian (c. 160-225 AD) in his *De Praescriptione*. Tertullian's views are in stark contrast with St. Thomas Aquinas who had such high regard for Aristotle that he called him "the Philosopher." In distinguishing proper speculative theology from improper speculative theology, an important distinction Tertullian does not make, the noted Thomist philosopher Peter Kreeft

---

[151] "Philip," Etymology Online, http://etymonline.com/index.php?allowed_in_frame=0&search=philip&searchmode=none; "Andrew," Etymology Online, http://etymonline.com/index.php?allowed_in_frame=0&search=andrew&searchmode=none.

explains in reference to Aquinas, "Christians have concrete data (in divine revelation) as well as abstract speculation (in philosophizing and theologizing), and the speculation must conform to the data. If it does, it can really prove such things, just as the sciences do with their data. St. Thomas also is careful to humbly distinguish such only-probable arguments, which are only from 'fittingness', from certain demonstrations."[152]

~ Tertullian on Greek Philosophy and "Wretched Aristotle" ~

Wretched Aristotle! who established for them the dialectic art, so ingenious in the construction and refutation of propositions, so crafty in statements, so forced in hypotheses, so inflexible in arguments, so laborious in disputes, so damaging even to itself, always reconsidering everything, so that it never treats thoroughly of anything at all.

Hence come those fables and endless genealogies, and profitless questions, and words which spread like a cancer; in restraining us from which the Apostle expressly mentions philosophy as that which we ought to beware of, writing to the Colossians, "Take heed lest

---

[152] Peter Kreeft, Practical Theology: Spiritual Direction from Saint Thomas Aquinas (San Francisco: Ignatius Press, 2014), 327.

anyone beguile you through philosophy or vain deceit, according to the tradition of men," beyond the providence of the Holy Spirit. The Apostle had been at Athens, and in his argumentative encounters there had become acquainted with that human wisdom which affects and corrupts the Truth, itself also being many times divided into its own heresies by the variety of its mutually antagonistic sects.

What then hath Athens in common with Jerusalem? What hath the Academy in common with the Church? What have heretics in common with Christians? Our principles are from the "Porch" of Solomon, who himself handed down that the Lord must be sought in simplicity of heart. Away with those who bring forward a Stoic or Platonic or dialectic Christianity. We have no need of speculative inquiry after we have known Christ Jesus; nor of search for the Truth after we have received the Gospel. When we become believers, we have no desire to believe anything besides; for the first article of our belief is that there is nothing besides which we ought to believe.[153]

Unlike Aquinas, Tertullian is not recognized by the

---

[153] Tertullian, "On the 'Prescription' of Heretics," trans. T. Herbert Bindley (London: Society for Promoting Christian Doctrine, 1914), chap. vii, 45-, *Tertullian Project*, http://www.tertullian.org/articles/bindley_test/bindley_test_07prae.htm.

Catholic Church as a saint, nor did he lead an exemplary life. He was drawn to the heretical group called Montanism, named after its founder Montanus (c. 135 - ?). Montanus' heretical teaching was supported by two women "prophets," Priscilla and Maximilla, who were his most prominent followers. Montanus and his prophets rejected Church authority. They argued that all that was needed was the prophetic inspiration of the Holy Spirit.[154]

Rome and Christianity

It has been noted that Judaism provided Christian civilization with its soul, and the Greeks with its intellect. Both of these aspects "when the fullness of the time came" (Galatians 4:4 NASB) were fulfilled, according to Catholic faith, in Christ. We will now move on to the third civilization which also contributed to Christianity. Roman law and order, concretely evident in their political structures, influenced the development of order in the Church, specifically regarding Church canon law and the division of ecclesial territory. The Church term of a diocese comes directly from Emperor Diocletian who in 293 divided his empire into four ways called a Tetrarchy, which were further

---

[154] Joseph Francis Kelly, *History and Heresy: How Historical Forces Can Create Doctrinal Conflicts* (Collegeville: Liturgical Press, 2012), 29-32.

Chapter 8: Early Christian Civilization

subdivided into dioceses.[155] Other aspects from Roman civilization that were taken up by Christianity include the Latin language, and Roman architecture, specifically the basilica, which you were introduced to in a previous chapter. When comparing the two diagrams below notice how Christianity transformed the Roman Basilica by making it into a cross shape.

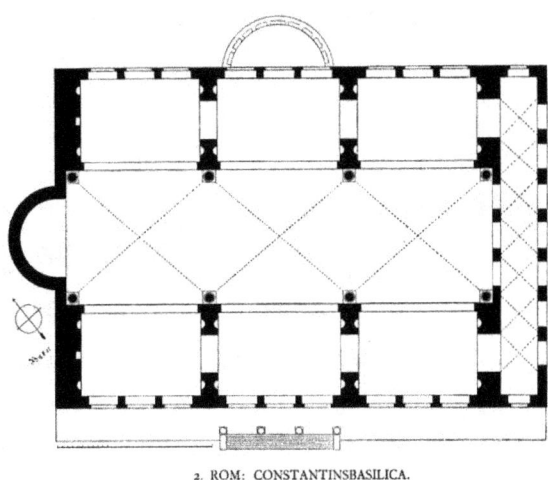

2. ROM: CONSTANTINSBASILICA.

~ Diagram of a Roman Basilica ~[156]

---

[155] Many historians maintain that Diocletian promoted Maximian the second.

[156] "Floor plan of the Basilica of Maxentius and Constantine," floorplan, http://commons.wikimedia.org/wiki/File:Dehio_6_Basilica_of_Maxentius_Floor_plan.jpg. 178 Lusitana, "Floor plan of a Christian church of basilical form, with the transept shaded." http://en.wikipedia.org/ wiki/File:Transept.png

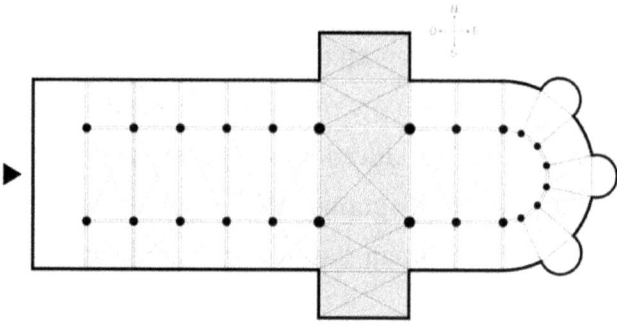

~ Diagram of a Christian Basilica ~[157]

Christianity in Roman History

The oldest non-biblical references to Christianity are from two Roman historians Tacitus (c. 58-116 AD), and Suetonius (c. 70-122 AD), and one Roman governmental official, Pliny the Younger (c. 61 - c. 113 AD). Below are key excerpts from their writings.

~ Tacitus on Christ ~

Consequently, to get rid of the report, Nero fastened the guilt and inflicted the most exquisite tortures on a class hated for their abominations, called Christians by the populace. *Christus*, from whom the name had its

---

[157] "Querhaus," Wikimedia, https://commons.wikimedia.org/wiki/File:Querhaus.svg

origin, suffered the extreme penalty during the reign of Tiberius at the hands of one of our procurators, Pontius Pilatus, and a most mischievous superstition, thus checked for the moment, again broke out not only in *Judæa*, the first source of the evil, but even in Rome, where all things hideous and shameful from every part of the world find their center and become popular. Accordingly, an arrest was first made of all who pleaded guilty; then, upon their information, an immense multitude was convicted, not so much of the crime of firing the city, as of hatred against mankind. Mockery of every sort was added to their deaths. Covered with the skins of beasts, they were torn by dogs and perished, or were nailed to crosses, or were doomed to the flames and burnt, to serve as a nightly illumination, when daylight had expired. Nero offered his gardens for the spectacle....[158]

~ Suetonius on Christ ~

He [Emperor Claudius Caesar (reigned 41-54 AD)] allowed the people of Ilium perpetual exemption from tribute, on the ground that they were the founders of the Roman race, reading an ancient letter of the senate and people of Rome written in Greek to king Seleucus, in

---

[158] Tacitus, *Annals and Histories*, trans. Alfred John Church, (New York: Alfred A. Knopf, 2009), 353-354.

which they promised him their friendship and alliance only on condition that he should keep their kinsfolk of Ilium free from every burden. Since the Jews constantly made disturbances at the instigation of *Chrestus*, he expelled them from Rome.[159]

~ Pliny the Younger on Christians ~

…They asserted, however, that the sum and substance of their fault or error had been that they were accustomed to meet on a fixed day before dawn and sing responsively a hymn to Christ as to a god, and to bind themselves by oath, not to some crime, but not to commit fraud, theft, or adultery, not falsify their trust, nor to refuse to return a trust when called upon to do so. When this was over, it was their custom to depart and to assemble again to partake of food - but ordinary and innocent food. Even this, they affirmed, they had ceased to do after my edict by which, in accordance with your instructions, I had forbidden political associations. Accordingly, I judged it all the more necessary to find out what the truth was by torturing two female slaves who were called deaconesses.

---

[159] Gaius Suetonius, "*The Lives of the Twelve Caesars,*" trans. J.C. Rolfe, *Claudius*, 25, University of Chicago, http://penelope.uchicago.edu/Thayer/E/Roman/Texts/Suetonius/12Caesars/Claudius*.html

But I discovered nothing else but depraved, excessive superstition....[160]

Quiz 8 for Chapter 8

1. According to Revelation 21, which city is most essential in forming a distinctly Christian civilization?

2-4. Who was Titus Flavius Josephus? In answering this question include the following: *Jewish Antiquities*, Jesus, and John the Baptist.

5. Explain Jesus' relationship with the Joshua of the Old Testament.

6-7. As explained in the chapter, were Jesus and Peter members of the lowest economic class? In answering this question include the trades of a *tekton* and a fisherman.

---

[160] Pliny the Younger, "*Pliny to the Emperor Trajan Letters 10.96-97,*" Georgetown, http://faculty.georgetown.edu/jod/texts/pliny.html.

6.

7.

8-10. As explained in the chapter, explain Jesus' and his Twelve Apostles' mission in relationship to the prophet Elijah's mission.

8.

9.

10.

11-13. Name three ways where Jesus's way of life was considered jarring by many Jewish people.

11.

12.

13.

14. As explained in the chapter, what did the adoption of Greek philosophical terms allow Christians to do with the particularity of Jewish ideas?

Chapter 8: Early Christian Civilization 181

15-16. Why did Tertullian call Aristotle "wretched" and assert that "We have no need of speculative inquiry after we have known Christ Jesus"? Are these beliefs of his in accordance with the Catholic approach to Greek philosophy and speculative inquiry?

15.

16.

17-19. Name three aspects from Roman civilization that Christianity adopted.

17.

18.

19.

Chapter 9

Fall of Rome and the Rise of Christianity

Introduction

After a few centuries of persecution of Christians by Roman Emperors, followed by period of relative harmony between Christianity and Roman rulers, Rome was sacked in 410 AD by the Visigothic leader Alaric I. Finally, in 476 AD, the barbarian Odoacer removed the last Roman Emperor from his throne, Emperor Romulus Augustus (nicknamed Romulus Augustulus meaning little Augustus).[161]

The two book ends of the Roman Empire were its first emperor the great Caesar Augustus (reigned 27-14 AD) and its last emperor the "little Augustus" Romulus Augustulus (reigned 475-476 AD). After the little Augustus was deposed, the Roman Empire ceased to officially exist. Pagans who deemed themselves as conservators of Roman traditions blamed Christianity for Rome's fall. According to them Rome fell because Christianity virtually ended the worship

---

[161] Adrian Keith Goldsworthy, *How Rome Fell: Death of a Superpower* (New Haven: Yale University Press, 2009), 11.

of the traditional gods.[162] For this reason, explains Ratzinger:

> When Christianity was looking in the Roman world for a word with which it could express, in a synthetic way understandable to everyone, what Jesus Christ meant to them, it came across the word *conservator*, which had designated in Rome the essential duty and the highest service necessary to render to mankind. But this very title the Christians could not and would not transfer to their Redeemer; with that term, indeed they could not translate the word Messiah or Christ or describe the task of the Savior of the World...The fact that Christ could be described not as *Conservator*, but as *Salvator* certainly had no political or revolutionary significance, but nevertheless indicated the limits of mere conservatism and pointed to a dimension of human life that goes beyond the causes of peace and order, which are the proper subject of politics.[163]

Christianity indirectly brought an end to traditional Roman religion by refusing that the Triune God be con-

---

[162] J.H.W.F. Liebeschuetz, *East and West in Late Antiquity: Invasion, Settlement, Ethnogenesis and Conflicts of Religion* (Leiden: Brill, 2015), 405.

[163] Joseph Ratzinger, *Europe, Today and Tomorrow*, trans. Michael J. Miller (San Francisco: Ignatius Press, 2004), 48-49.

sidered by the Romans as just one more God. For this reason, Christians forbade the Triune God to be represented in the Roman building dedicated to all the gods, called the Pantheon. Their refusal, explains Ratzinger, "exploded antiquity's idea of tolerance" that was represented by the Pantheon as "a space for religious tolerance through the exchange and mutual recognition of gods."[164]

This lack of tolerance on the part of Christians enraged Roman conservatives. They interpreted the refusal as signifying that Christianity was a rival religion to the worship of multiple gods approved by the Roman state. When Emperor Constantine with the 313 AD Edict of Milan allowed Christianity to freely practice and when he accepted baptism on his death bed,[165] Christians were given great motivation to bring an end to the Roman worship of many gods. Soon, Christianity overtook and replaced the Roman religion, and spread a Christian culture, essentially formed by the "cult" of Christ.

---

[164] Joseph Cardinal Ratzinger, *Church, Ecumenism & Politics*, trans. Michael J. Miller (San Francisco: Ignatius Press, 2008), 201.

[165] John Chapman, "Eusebius of Nicomedia," *The Catholic Encyclopedia*, Vol. 5 (New York: Robert Appleton Company, 1909), New Advent, http://www.newadvent.org/cathen/05623b.htm; R. Joseph Hoffmann, *Julian's Against the Galileans* (Amherst: Prometheus Books, 2004), 12-35.

As explained by the New Testament scripture scholar Bart D. Eherman, "The religions [Roman religions at the time of Constantine] were called cults not because they were dangerous and marginalized; the word cult is simply an abbreviated form of the term *cultus deorum*, Latin for 'care of the gods' (just as agriculture is 'care of the fields'). These religions were concerned with caring for the gods so that the gods would, in exchange, care for the people."[166] The Christian "cult" only cared about the one true God of revelation, while rightly deeming all other gods as false. We will now study a few essential elements that make up the Christian culture that for centuries was at the heart of Western Civilization: beliefs (the true), worship (the beautiful), and practice (the good).[167]

Christian Belief: The True

After Jesus died, Christian belief developed with the aid of the Holy Spirit as Jesus promised, "I will ask the Father, and he will give you another Advocate, to be with you forever. This is the Spirit of truth, whom the world cannot receive, because it neither sees him nor knows him. You know

---

[166] Bart D. Ehrman, *The New Testament*, Transcript Book (Chantilly: The Great Courses, 2000), 21.

[167] Peter Kreeft, *Practical Theology: Spiritual Direction from Saint Thomas Aquinas* (San Francisco: Ignatius Press, 2014), ix.

him, because he abides with you, and he will be in you." (John 14: 16-18 NRSV)

One principal way in which Christian belief developed was by inspired authors, beginning with St. Paul's 1st Letter to the Thessalonians, writing down the New Testament. In time, as explained by Benedict XVI, "together with 'apostolic succession', the early Church discovered (she did *not* invent) two further elements fundamental for her unity: the canon of Scripture and the so-called *regula fidei*, or 'rule of faith'."[168]

The Holy Spirit helped the Church to discern which books were to form the canon of inspired scripture and which were not. The Church, by means of the Holy Spirit, acted as an ultimate authority when determining the canon. However, the inspired message of Sacred Scripture acts as an ultimate authority to which the Church is at service. As *Dei Verbum* of the Second Vatican Council states, "This teaching office [of the Church] is not above the word of God, but serves it, teaching only what has been handed on, listening to it devoutly, guarding it scrupulously and explaining it faithfully in accord with a divine commission and with the help of the Holy Spirit, it draws from this one deposit of faith everything which it presents for belief as divinely re-

---

[168] Benedict XVI, *Jesus of Nazareth Holy Week: From the Entrance into Jerusalem to the Resurrection* (San Francisco: Ignatius Press, 2011), 99.

vealed."[169]

That Sacred Scripture, Tradition, and the Authority of the Church are mutually subordinate to one another due to their participation in Divine Truth is also clearly stated by *Dei Verbum*, "It is clear, therefore, that sacred tradition, Sacred Scripture and the teaching authority of the Church, in accord with God's most wise design, are so linked and joined together that one cannot stand without the others, and that all together and each in its own way under the action of the one Holy Spirit contribute effectively to the salvation of souls."[170] The inspired books of the canon of Sacred Scripture do not, therefore, function alone as a sole authority but together with Tradition and the Magisterium share authority.

Another way of stating this is that, with respect to the message of Sacred Scripture, the teaching authority of the Church and Tradition are subordinate to Scripture. However, with respect to the text that carries the inspired message, the Magisterium and Tradition have an interpretive, authoritative role in order to understand and convey the message as God intends. The obscurity of certain passages of Sacred Scripture that require the interpretive role of the

---

[169] Vatican II, *Dei Verbum*, 1965, chap. 2, no. 10, http://www.vatican.va/archive/hist_councils/ii_vatican_council/documents/vat-ii_const_19651118_dei-verbum_ en.html.

[170] Vatican II, *Dei Verbum*, 1965, chap. 2, no. 10.

Church is testified by Peter, "So also our beloved brother Paul wrote to you according to the wisdom given him, speaking of this as he does in all his letters. There are some things in them hard to understand, which the ignorant and unstable twist to their own destruction, as they do the other scriptures. You therefore, beloved, since you are forewarned, beware that you are not carried away with the error of the lawless and lose your own stability." (2 Peter 3:15-17 NRSV)

The earliest example of the Church fulfilling her role as authority over the text of Sacred Scripture to be of service to the authority of the inspired message of Sacred Scripture were rules of faith, referred to by Benedict XVI. The rules of faith consisted of short summaries of the faith that were especially used in the early Church during baptismal confessions of faith. According to Benedict XVI, "This rule of faith, or creed, constitutes the real 'hermeneutic' of Scripture, the key derived from Scripture itself by which the sacred text can be interpreted according to its spirit."[171]

Christian Worship: The Beautiful

As the Christian understanding of the spiritually true developed, so did their integration of these truths in the

---

[171] Benedict XVI, *Jesus of Nazareth Holy Week: From the Entrance into Jerusalem to the Resurrection* (San Francisco: Ignatius Press, 2011), 99.

spiritually beautiful.[172] The Christian culture that was, and to some extent still is, at the heart of Western Civilization was formed by this development in worship. The doorway into Christian culture was the liturgical celebration of baptism. This sacrament was seen as of such great importance that babies along with entire households were baptized.[173] In time, a formal process of pre-baptismal instruction called the catechumenate was instituted by the Church. The practice of the catechumenate disappeared during medieval times. It was reinstated in 1965 by the Second Vatican Council.

Faith in baptismal practices have given Christians a renewed and deepened sense of being made in the image and likeness of God as Genesis reveals. Pope St. Leo the Great (reigned 440-461 AD) explains, "Through the sacrament of baptism you have become a temple of the Holy Spirit. Do not drive away so great a guest by evil conduct and become again a slave to the devil, for your liberty was bought by the blood of Christ."[174]

Another saint from early Christian history, St. John Chrysostom (c. 349-407 AD), additionally explains that bap-

---

[172] Peter Kreeft, *Practical Theology: Spiritual Direction from Saint Thomas Aquinas* (San Francisco: Ignatius Press, 2014), ix.

[173] Acts 16:15, Acts 16:33, 1 Cor. 1:16.

[174] Pope St. Leo the Great, "Sermo 1 in Nativitate Domini, 1-3: PL 54, 190-193" in The Liturgy of the Hours, Vol. I (New York: Catholic Book Publishing Co., 1975), 405.

tism is intricately related to another foundational sacrament, the Eucharist. He writes, "There flowed from his [Jesus'] side water and blood. Beloved, do not pass over this mystery without thought; it has yet another hidden meaning, which I will explain to you. I said that water and blood symbolized baptism and the holy Eucharist. From these two sacraments the Church is born..."[175]

First Century Christian Chapel in Damascus, Syria[176]

---

[175] John Chrysostom "Catechesis 3, 3-19: SC 50, 174-177," in The Liturgy of the Hours, vol II (New York: Catholic Book Publishing Co.,1976), 474.

[176] Titoni Thomas, "Chapel of Saint Ananias, Damascus, Syria, an early example of a Christian house of worship; built in the 1st century AD," https://commons.wikimedia.org/wiki/File%3AInside_of_Saint_Ananias.jpg.

Christian Ethics: The Good

The belief in being called by God to be living temples of the Holy Spirit and tabernacles of Jesus Christ had a profound affect in how Christians conceived of what is spiritually good.[177] A practical ethical consequence of this belief is the consistent Christian defense of the sacredness of human life from the moment of conception to natural death. Roman pagans noticed the Christians' unique view of human life. The second century *Epistle of Mathetes to Diognetus* by a pagan Roman describes Christians as not like others since they marry but do not kill their babies nor commit adultery, they obey Roman law but in a way that surpasses the law, and they honor the name of others. To truly live out Western Civilization as it is in its essence is to make prominent and to allow these characteristics of early Christian life to flourish.

Chapter V - The Manners of the Christians.

For the Christians are distinguished from other men neither by country, nor language, nor the customs which they observe. For they neither inhabit cities of their own, nor employ a peculiar form of speech, nor lead a life

---

[177] Peter Kreeft, *Practical Theology: Spiritual Direction from Saint Thomas Aquinas* (San Francisco: Ignatius Press, 2014), ix.

which is marked out by any singularity. The course of conduct which they follow has not been devised by any speculation or deliberation of inquisitive men; nor do they, like some, proclaim themselves the advocates of any merely human doctrines. But, inhabiting Greek as well as barbarian cities, according as the lot of each of them has determined, and following the customs of the natives in respect to clothing, food, and the rest of their ordinary conduct, they display to us their wonderful and confessedly striking method of life. They dwell in their own countries, but simply as sojourners. As citizens, they share in all things with others, and yet endure all things as if foreigners. Every foreign land is to them as their native country, and every land of their birth as a land of strangers. They marry, as do all [others]; they beget children; but they do not destroy their offspring. They have a common table, but not a common bed. They are in the flesh, but they do not live after the flesh. They pass their days on earth, but they are citizens of heaven. They obey the prescribed laws, and at the same time surpass the laws by their lives. They love all men, and are persecuted by all. They are unknown and condemned; they are put to death, and restored to life. They are poor, yet make many rich; they are in lack of all things, and yet abound in all; they are dishonored, and yet in their very dishonor are glorified. They are evil spoken of, and yet are justified; they are reviled, and bless; they are insulted, and repay the insult with honor; they do good, yet are punished as evil-doers. When punished, they rejoice as if quickened into life; they are assailed by the Jews as foreigners, and are persecuted by the Greeks; yet those who hate them are unable to assign any reason for their hatred.[178]

Quiz 9 for Chapter 9

1-4. Why did Roman *conservatores* blame Christianity for Rome's fall? Include in your answer the following: gods, Triune God, Pantheon, and tolerance.

5. Why did Christians chose the title *Salvator* and not *Conservator* for Christ?

---

[178] "The Epistle of Mathetes to Diognetus," •Roberts-Donaldson English Translation, Early Christian Writings, http://www.earlychristianwritings.com/text/diognetus-roberts.html.

Chapter 9: Fall of Rome and the Rise of Christianity 195

6-9. What are three principal ways in which the spiritually true is defined by Christianity? In answering this question include the concept of mutual subordination.

10. How were the truths of Christianity formed sacramentally by the spiritual beautiful?

11-15. In their practice of goodness, how did Christians differ from the Roman pagan understanding of human life? In answering this question, include reference to *Epistle of Mathetes to Diognetus*, babies, marriage, law, and reputation.

Chapter 10

Medieval World

Introduction

After pagan Rome fell, the Roman Western world was civilized and evangelized by the Catholic Church. In doing so, Western Civilization became grounded in a culture formed in the heart of the Church, argues Thomas E. Woods in *How the Catholic Church Built Western Civilization*. The medieval time in which this occurred was far from being a supposedly dark time but rather one full of light, and creativity. During the medieval age, writes Wood:

> The university system a gift of Western civilization to the world, was developed by the Catholic Church. Historians have marveled at the extent to which intellectual debate in those universities was free and unfettered. The exaltation of human reason and its capabilities, a commitment to rigorous and rational debate, a promotion of intellectual inquiry and scholarly exchange – all sponsored by the Church – provided the framework for the Scientific

Revolution....[179]

Through the perspective of the Medieval Era of being one of light, creativity, and the promotion of human reason, we will look at medieval education, science, guilds, literature, and art. This is not to say that the Medieval Era did not have its share of darkness that all ages contain. But instead of highlighting these aspects, which of course includes the horrific Black Death also known as the Bubonic Plague that claimed millions of lives in Europe in the mid fourteenth century, we will focus on the more inspiring aspects of medieval life.

A way for defining the beginning and end of the medieval way of life can be from 476 AD to 1453 AD, which is from when the last Western Roman Emperor was deposed and Rome's power came to an end, signaling the end of antiquity and the end of the early Christian era, to when the capital of the Eastern Roman empire, Constantinople, was defeated by the Ottoman, Islamic Empire.

Medieval Education

In the early medieval age, a primary way, but not only

---

[179] Thomas E. Woods, *How the Catholic Church Built Western Civilization* (Washington, D.C.: Regnery Publishing, 2012), 4.

way, where Catholics were educated beyond catechetical instruction was in monasteries. There were also clerical, non-monastic schools.[180] As cities developed, bishops began improving their Cathedral schools to more effectively educate their clergy. Soon, the demand for education surpassed what the Cathedral schools could offer. This led to the founding of a new model of education, the university. In 1155, the Holy Roman Emperor Frederick I Barbarossa greatly helped this new educational model to develop by issuing the constitution *Authentica Habita*. The constitution document allowed students and scholars to travel with less impediment to study in foreign lands. If they acquired debt during the time of their studies, the constitution required they were to be treated justly. They were further protected by the option of being tried by their teachers or in the courts of the local bishop.[181]

A notable example of an early university was the University of Paris (*La Sorbonne*), established around 1231. Pope Gregory IX gave formal recognition of the university's

---

[180] Jean Leclercq, *The Love of Learning and the Desire for God: A Study of Monastic Culture*, trans. Catherine Misrahi (New York: Fordham University press, 1982), 193-194.

[181] Hilde de Ridder-Symoens, *A History of the University in Europe: Volume 1, Universities in the Middle Ages* (Cambridge: Cambridge University Press, 1992), 78.

self-governance in his papal bull, *Parens Scientiarum*.[182] Across Europe similarly structured universities were also founded. The universities were organized in a way similar to the guild system, which we will discuss later. The teachers acted as the masters with the students as apprentices.

The curriculum of the universities, originally from classical antiquity, broke up education according to two categories: quality and quantity. That which is highly quantifiable was called the *quadrivium*, which in Latin means four ways, or four roads. The *quadrivium* consisted of arithmetic, geometry, astronomy, and music. In addition to subjects that focused on quantity, subjects that emphasized quality were also studied. These were called the *trivium* and included grammar, rhetoric, and logic. During the middle of the 1200s, these ways to wisdom were supplemented by philosophical studies, namely natural, metaphysical, and moral. Universities distinguished themselves from others by emphasizing some of the ways over others. For example, the University of Oxford focused on natural philosophy more than the University of Paris did. The University of Paris was known for its metaphysics and logic.[183]

---

[182] de Ridder-Symoens, 23, 89, 90, 422.
[183] de Ridder-Symoens, 308-309.

Quadrivium	Trivium
Arithmetic	Grammar
Geometry	Logic
Astronomy	Rhetoric
Music	

The systematic way of study at the universities is commonly called scholasticism. While a development of the ancient monastic educational model, the scholastic system of education was quite different in a number of key ways. Monastic education was undertaken primarily for personal spiritual growth. Life and study, therefore, were to be integrated. The scholastic model, in contrast, with its emphasis on abstract, theoretical knowledge, studied in a systematic, logical, and highly rational manner, tended to separate study from life.[184] In describing this integration of learning, or the love of letters with sanctification, the noted scholar Jean Leclercq in *The Love of Learning and the Desire for God* writes:

> Monastic culture of the Middle Ages has two kinds of sources. Some are of literary nature: written texts whose content must be assimilated through meditative reading or through study. Others belong to the domain of reli-

---

[184] Leclercq, *The Love of Learning and the Desire for God*, 20, 22, 53.

gious experience. Of these latter, the most important, the one which enables all the others to be combined in the harmony of a synthesis, is the one which induces the desire to reach the culmination of this experience. The content of monastic culture has seemed to be symbolized, synthesized, by these two words: grammar and spirituality. On the one hand, learning is necessary if one is to approach God and to express what is perceived of Him; on the other hand, literature must be continually transcended and elevated in the striving to attain eternal life.[185]

Simply because scholastic education did not as clearly integrate academics with growth in holiness, does not mean, though, that the scholastic model could not as well be integrated with growth in sanctity. A few examples of great scholastics and saints are the Dominicans St. Albert the Great (1200-1280) and St. Thomas Aquinas (1225-1274), and the Franciscan St. Bonaventure (1221-1274). Albert the Great taught Aquinas who studied at the University of Paris along with Bonaventure.

Medieval Science

Scientific discoveries flourished during the Medieval

---

[185] Leclercq, 53.

Age. A main reason for this is the Judeo-Christian belief in a God who out of nothing created the world. Since God created the world, the world bears within it an intelligent design of its divine author and His uncreated intellect. By being made in God's image and likeness (Genesis 1:26), men and women are also intelligent and, therefore, with their created intellects can decipher the intelligent design of the world instilled in it by God. As Benedict XVI wrote, "man can re-think the *logos*, the meaning of being, because his own *logos*, his own reason, is *logos* of the one *logos*, thought of the original thought, of the creative spirit that permeates and governs his being."[186]

Acceptance and faith in a creating God who Himself is uncreated leads to the conclusion that what He created is not divine with a mind and/or unpredictable will of its own but instead unfolds according to the providential designs of God's mind. The intelligent unfolding of the world is another way of saying that there are laws within the world that are capable of being discovered scientifically by the human mind.

A few notable examples of people encouraged by their faith to make scientific discoveries include the following. The English bishop Robert Grosseteste (1168-1253) examined light in an empirical manner, preparing the way for

---

[186] Joseph Cardinal Ratzinger, *Introduction to Christianity*, trans. J.R. Foster (San Francisco: Ignatius Press, 1990), 32.

his student Roger Bacon's scientific method. The French bishop Nicholas Oresme (1329-1392) was an accomplished mathematician who studied motion including the rotation of the earth. The Dominican German bishop St. Albert the Great (1200-1280) was a botanist and zoologist. The English Archbishop Thomas Bradwardine (1290-1349) proposed a law for falling objects. The German Cardinal Nicholas of Cusa (1401-1464) was a skilled mathematician and astronomer. The Franciscan Friar Roger Bacon (c.1214-1294) developed an empirically based methodology for studying creation. Prior to Galileo, the Polish canon Nicolaus Copernicus (1473-1543) provided evidence for the heliocentric theory, but, unlike Galileo, Copernicus did so in a respectful and cautious manner that did not unduly upset Church officials.[187]

Since a woman medieval scientist has not been mentioned, we will conclude with Saint Hildegard of Bingen, O.S.B. (1098-1179). St. Hildegard of Bingen was a German Benedictine abbess who demonstrated proficiency not only in theology and philosophy but also in botany and in medicine.[188] In recognition of her significant contributions Pope Benedict XVI named St. Hildegard a Doctor of the Church

---

[187] Christopher T. Baglow, *Faith, Science & Reason* (Woodridge: Midwest Theological Forum, 2009), 68-70.

[188] Fiona Maddocks, *Hildegard of Bingen: The Woman of Her Age* (New York: Doubleday, 2001), 124, 149-150, 157.

on 7 October, 2012.[189]

Medieval Guilds

The medieval age was not only one of individual scientific achievement and enlightenment propelled by the enlightenment given by faith, but it also was an age in which people gathered to care for one another communally. This forming of protective and caring associations is in accordance with early Christian life recorded in Acts chapter two, verse forty-five, "They would sell their possessions and goods and distribute the proceeds to all, as any had need." (NRSV) According to Tertullian (160-220), the Romans noticed this unique Christian love and would at times say in astonishment, "See, how they love one another."[190] The early Christian Father St. Justin Martyr (100-165) similarly wrote:

---

[189] Benedict XVI, "Holy Mass for the Opening of the Synod of Bishops and Proclamation of St John of Avila and of St Hildegard of Bingen as Doctors of the Church," Oct. 7, 2012, http://www.vatican.va/holy_father/benedict_xvi/homilies/2012/documents/hf_ben-xvi_hom_20121007_apertura-sinodo_en.html

[190] Tertullian, "The Apology," trans, S. Thelwall, chap. 34, no. 7, *The Tertullian Project*, Christian Classics Ethereal Library, http://www.tertullian.org/anf/anf03/footnote/fn2.htm#P254_53171.

[W]e who formerly delighted in fornication, but now embrace chastity alone; we who formerly used magical arts, dedicate ourselves to the good and unbegotten God; we who valued above all things the acquisition of wealth and possessions, now bring what we have into a common stock, and communicate to everyone in need....[191]

Workers of the medieval age expressed the pronounced Christian communal tendency by forming themselves into guilds that not only controlled quality but also provided a protective, Christian environment. The following statues of a Southampton English Guild explicitly state what this communal security entailed.

---

[191] Justin Martyr concludes with, "we who hated and destroyed one another, and on account of their different manners would not live with men of a different tribe, now, since the coming of Christ, live familiarly with them, and pray for our enemies, and endeavor to persuade those who hate us unjustly to live conformably to the good precepts of Christ, to the end that they may become partakers with us of the same joyful hope of a reward from God the ruler of all." Justin Martyr, "The Apostolic Fathers with Justin Martyr and Irenaeus by Philip Schaff," *The First Apology*, chap. 14, The Christian Classics Ethereal Library, http://www.ccel.org/ccel/schaff/anf01.viii.ii.xiv.html?highlight=hate,and,destroy#highlight.

Southampton Guild Organization, 14th Century

...

4. And when the gild shall sit, the lepers of La Madeleine shall have of the alms of the gild, two sesters (approximately eight gallons) of ale, and the sick of God's House and of St. Julian shall have two sesters of ale. And the Friars Minors shall have two sesters of ale and one sester of wine. And four sesters of ale shall be given to the poor wherever the gild shall meet.

...

6. And when the gild sits, and any guildsman is outside of the city so that he does not know when it will happen, he shall have a gallon of wine, if his servants come to get it. And if a guildsman is ill and is in the city, wine shall be sent to him, two loaves of bread and a gallon of wine and a dish from the kitchen; and two approved men of the gild shall go to visit him and look after his condition.

7. And when a guildsman dies, all those who are of the gild and are in the city shall attend the service of the dead, and the guildsmen shall bear the body and bring it to the place of burial. And whoever will not do this shall pay according to his oath, two pence, to be given to the poor. And those of the ward where the dead man shall be ought to find a man to watch

over the body the night that the dead shall lie in his house. And so long as the service of the dead shall last, that is to say the vigil and the mass, there ought to burn four candles of the gild, each candle of two pounds weight or more, until the body is buried. And these four candles shall remain in the keeping of the steward of the gild.

...

22. If any guildsman falls into poverty and has not the wherewithal to live, and is not able to work or to provide for himself, he shall have one mark from the gild to relieve his condition-when the gild shall sit. No one of the gild nor of the franchise shall avow another's goods for his by which the custom of the city shall be injured. And if any one does so and is convicted, he shall lose the gild and the franchise; and the merchandise so avowed shall be forfeited to the king.[192]

---

[192] Fordham University, *Medieval Sourcebook: Southampton Guild Organization, 14th Century*, Internet Medieval Source Book, http://www.fordham.edu/halsall/source/guild-sthhmptn.asp.

Medieval Literature and Medieval Visual Art

Major Christian inspired medieval work includes *The Canterbury Tales, The Poem of the Cid, The Song of Roland,* and *The Divine Comedy.*

The *Canterbury Tales* were written by the Englishman Geoffrey Chaucer (1343-1400). It describes stories pilgrims share as they travel to a shrine dedicated to St. Thomas Becket (1118-1170).

The late 12th or early 13th century Spanish *Poem of the Cid* is based on the life of a Catholic Spaniard, El Cid, who fought against Muslim rule.

The 11th or early 12th century *Song of Roland* is a French novel on the 778 Battle of Roncevaux Pass during the reign of Charlemagne.

The 14th century *Divine Comedy* by Dante Alighieri is a poem on Dante's being guided through Hell, Purgatory, and Heaven.

Much of medieval painting, influenced by Byzantine iconic art, is highly stylized and formal. Near the end of the medieval age, this style began to be modified by a more natural, flowing style. The artwork below is representative of these two styles.

Art of St. Mark's Basilica (c. late 1000s-1100s AD) Venice[193]

~ Italo-Byzantine Style ~

---

[193] "San Marco di Venezia, as seen from Piazza San Marco," http://commons.wikimedia.org/wiki/File%3AVeneza47.jpg; (next page) "St Mark's Basilica in Venice, where imported Byzantine mosaicists were succeeded by Italians they had trained," http://commons.wikimedia.org/wiki/File%3A Veneza 118.jpg, "Mosaic of the translation of the body of Saint Mark on San Alipio facade door of the Saint Mark's Basilica in Venice," http://commons.wikimedia.org/wiki/File%3A Mosaico_traslazione_San_Marco_Venezia.JPG, Dennis Jarvis, "The Pentecost Mosaic, in the center is the dove of the Holy Spirit with the twelve apostles below. This is one of the oldest mosaics in the church dating from 1125 AD," http://commons. wikimedia.org/wiki/File%3AVenice_SMarco_Vault2.jpg.

Chapter 10: Medieval World 211

194

¹⁹⁴ The Yorck Project: 10.000 Meisterwerke der Malerei. DVD-ROM, 2002. Distributed by DIRECTMEDIA Publishing

Chapter 10: Medieval World 213

The Florentine artist Cimabue (c. 1240-1302), along with other artists of his time including his student Giotto di Bondone (c. 1266–1337) began instilling more natural elements within the Italo-Byzantine style.[195]

(see next page)

GmbH, "10th-century gold and enamel Byzantine icon of St Michael, in the treasury," http://commons.wikimedia.org/wiki/File%3AMeister_der_Ikone_des_Erzengels_Michael_001_adjusted.jpg.

[195] Georgio Vasari, *The Lives of the Artists*, trans, Julia Conaway Bondanella (Oxford: Oxford University Press, 2008), 12; (pictured) Google Cultural Institute, "Cimabue's Maestà, 1280–1285, Uffizi Gallery, Florence," http://commons.wikimedia.org/wiki/File%3ACimabue_-_Maest%C3%A0_di_Santa_Trinita_-_Google_Art_Project.jpg; "Cimabue's Madonna di Castelfiorentino, 1280s," http://commons.Wikimedia.org/wiki/File%3ACimabue_madonna_castefliorentino.jpg; Starlight modified by GunnarBach, "Cimabue's Fresco in the Lower Basilica of Assisi," http://commons.wikimedia.org/wiki/File%3ASan_Francesco_Cimabue.jpg.

~ Cimabue's Art ~

Chapter 10: Medieval World 215

~ Giotto di Bondone's Art ~[196]

---

[196] Web Gallery of Art, "Giotto's Lamentation (The Mourning of Christ), Cappella degli Srovegni," http://commons.wikimedia.org/wiki/File%3AGiotto_-_Scrovegni_-_-36-_-_Lamentation_(The_Mourning_ of_Christ)_adj.jpg; The Yorck Project: *10.000 Meisterwerke der Malerei*. DVD-ROM, 2002, "Bardi Chapel: the Mourning of St. Francis," http://commons.wikimedia.org/wiki/File%3AGiotto_di_Bondone_060.jpg, DVDROM.

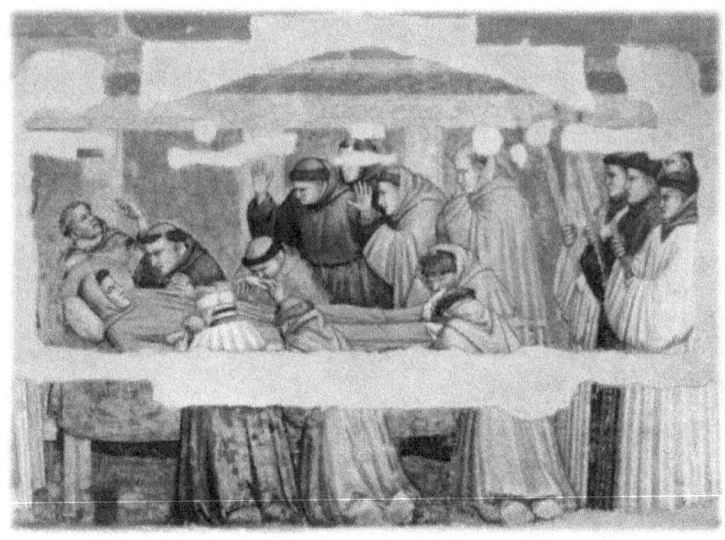

Quiz 10 for Chapter 10

1-4. Trace the development of medieval education. Include the following: monasteries, cathedrals, Frederick I Barbarossa, Pope Gregory IX.

5-14. Fill in the following chart representing a typical medieval curriculum.

Quadrivium	Trivium	Philosophy
5.	9.	12.
6.	10.	13.
7.	11.	14.
8.		

Chapter 10: Medieval World 217

6-7. Contrast the monastic educational model with the scholastic educational model.

6.

7.

8. Why did the Judeo-Christian belief in God and creation lay the groundwork for scientific discovery in the medieval age?

9. What was a main way, discussed in the chapter, that medieval artisans and craftsmen banded together to form protective associations? In answering this question describe in three specific ways how they loved and cared in these associations.

10-12. Identify, compare and contrast the following two works of art.

Chapter 11

Renaissance

Introduction

As the introduction to the previous chapter stated, 1453 is the date that can be loosely interpreted as the year when the Medieval Age ended and the Renaissance began. In 1453, the city of Constantinople was invaded by the Islamic, Ottoman Empire.

By defeating the capital of the Eastern Christian Empire, the Ottomans brought an end to the Eastern portion of the Roman Empire. (The Western portion of the Roman Empire had previously been overrun and subdued by European barbarians in the fifth century AD.)

The Greek intellectuals who fled from their defeated lands to the West brought with them their mastery of antiquity, in particular of Greek philosophy. This introduction of knowledge into the West was a factor in Western Civilization experiencing a rebirth which is what the term Renaissance means.

The exaltation of classical thought and practices of the Renaissance came to an end around the time of the French philosopher Rene Descartes, who is commonly considered as the founder of modern philosophy. His death in 1650 is a convenient date for identifying the end of the Renaissance and the beginning of the modern period, often called the Enlightenment. In this chapter, we will study Renaissance exploration, political centralization, literature, and art.

Age of Discovery

The fall of Constantinople not only helped to spark a re-appreciation of antiquity, but also motivated Europeans to discover new, cheaper trade routes, and, in the process, new lands. They were incentivized since the Ottoman Muslims who gained control over the Mediterranean coastal city of Constantinople charged Europeans a high price to cross over their lands.

Prior to 1453, European merchants traveled through land associated with Constantinople in order to reach the Silk Route. The Silk Route brought the merchants to Asian lands where they purchased goods to sell back home. A few of the important European discoverers are Henry the Navigator, King John II of Portugal, Bartolomeu Dias, Vasco de Gama, Christopher Columbus, Ferdinand Magellan, and John Cabot.

Chapter 11: Renaissance

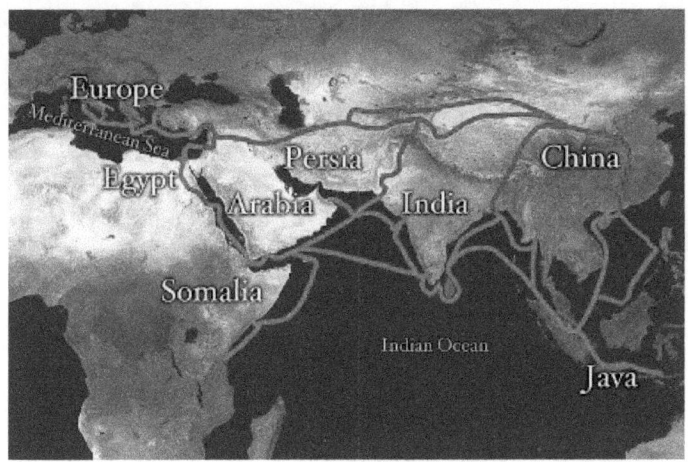

~ Silk Routes ~[197]

Prince Henry the Navigator (1394-1460) was a son of the Portuguese King John I. Inspired by a book about Marco Polo's travels to the Far East, Henry began financing Atlantic Ocean expeditions around Africa.[198]

---

[197] By Whole_world_-_land_and_oceans_12000.jpg: NASA/Goddard Space Flight Center derivative work:Splette derivative work:Bongan NASA - Visible Earth, images combined and scaled down by HighInBC (20 megabyte upload limit) NASA VIsible Earth [Public domain], via Wikimedia Commons, http://commons.wikimedia.org/wiki/File%3ASilk _route_copy.jpg.

[198] Peter Russell, *Prince Henry the Navigator* (New Haven: Yale University Press, 2001), 1-13; Ernle Bradford, *A Wind from the North: The Life of Henry the Navigator* (New York: Open Road Integrated Media Inc., 1960), 60.

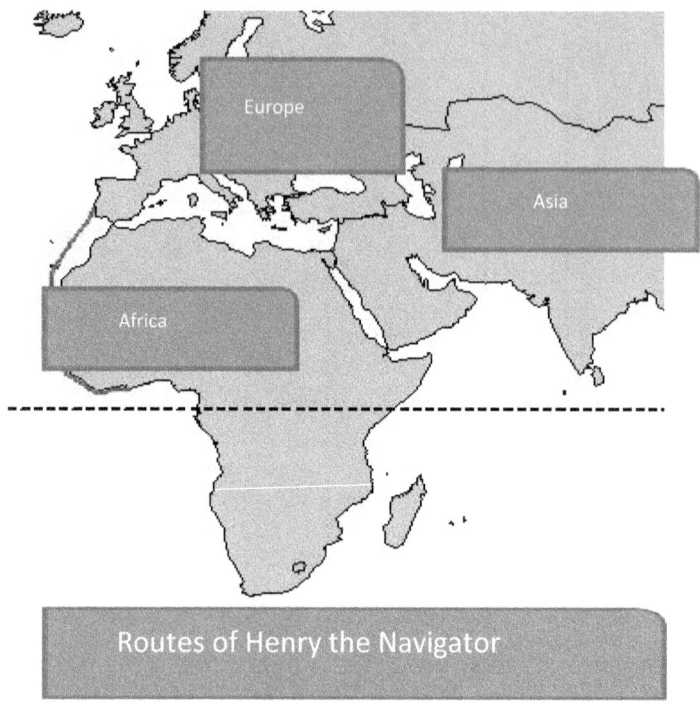

~ Navigation Routes Sponsored by Prince Henry ~[199]

King John II of Portugal (1455-1495) was also a patron of Portuguese explorers, intent on discovering Atlantic Ocean trade routes. Bartolomeu Dias (1451-1500) was one such explorer. In February of 1488, Dias sailed around the Southern tip of Africa to land in Mossel Bay.[200] In 1500, Dias

---

[199] Les routes d'Henri le Navigateur Auteur G. Dulous Mars 2007, http://commons.wikimedia.org/wiki/File:Routes_d%27 Henri_le_Navigateur.JPG#file

[200] A.R. Disney, *A History of Portugal and the Portuguese Empire: Volume Two, The Portuguese Empire* (Cambridge:

Chapter 11: Renaissance 223

and his ship were lost at sea.[201]

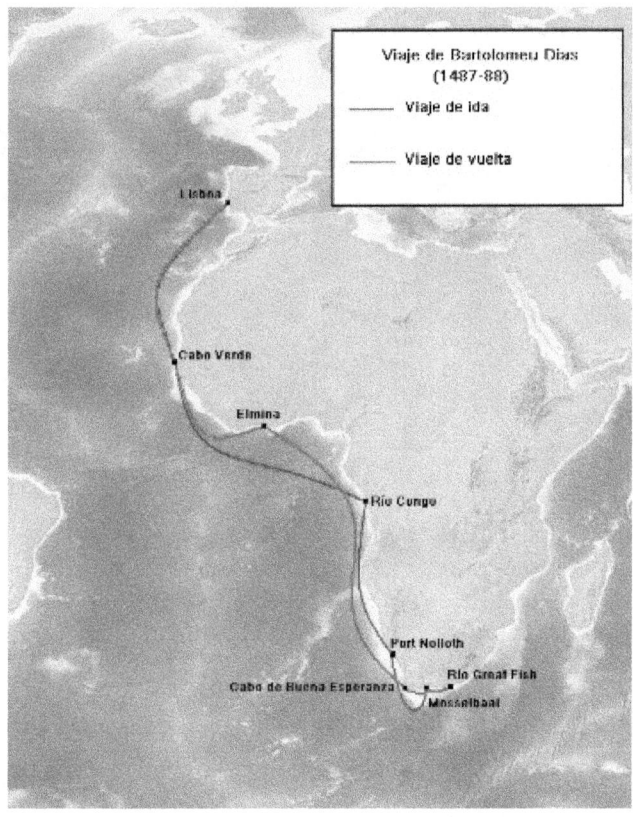

~ Expeditions of Bartolomeu Dias ~[202]

Following the routes set by Dias, the fellow Portuguese

Cambridge University Press, 2009), 38.

[201] James M. Anderson, *The History of Portugal* (Westport: Greenwood Press, 2000), 66.

[202] Wikimedia Commons, http://commons.wikimedia.org/wiki/File%3ABartolomeu_Dias_Voyage.PNG.

Vasco de Gama (c. 1460-1524) successfully sailed around Africa and, on May 18th, 1498, landed near Calcutta, India. His journey took over ten months to reach Calcutta and about eleven months on his way back to Lisbon.[203]

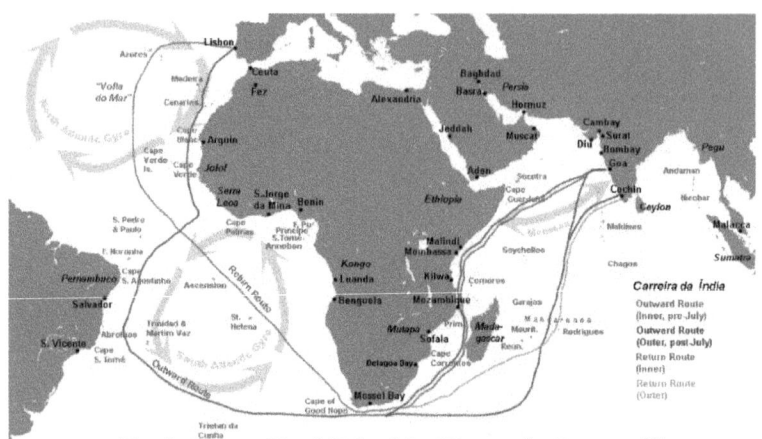

~ Trade Route Established by Vasco de Gama ~[204]

The next two explorers, Christopher Columbus and Ferdinand Magellan, sailed west instead of east with the hope of sailing around the globe to reach eastern lands. Columbus (c. 1450-1506) was an Italian explorer who unsuccessfully sought patronage from King John II Portugal. The Spanish monarchs, Isabella I and Ferdinand II, however, agreed to finance his expedition. In sailing westward, Columbus hit a large mass of land unknown to Europeans. He landed in the

---

[203] Disney, *A History of Portugal and the Portuguese Empire: Volume Two, The Portuguese Empire*, 121.

[204] Wikimedia Commons, http://commons.wikimedia.org/wiki/File%3AMap_of_Portuguese_Carreira_da_India.gif

Bahama Islands off the coast of this land and in both the central and southern parts of this massive land mass that the German mapmaker Martin Waldseemüller, in 1507, named America, after the Florentine map maker and explorer, Amerigo Vespucci.[205]

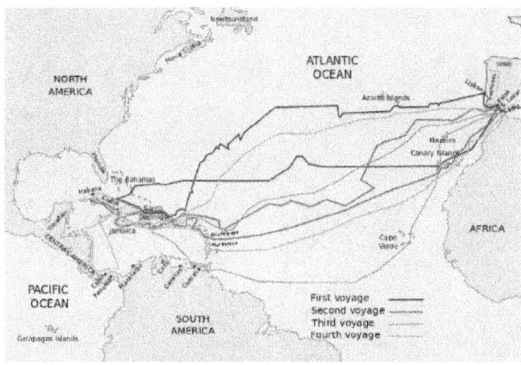

~ Journeys of Christopher Columbus ~ [206]

Like Columbus, the Portuguese explorer Ferdinand Magellan (c. 1480-1521) sought patronage from a Spanish monarch, King Charles I. Magellan also tried to sail west-

---

[205] Kirkpatrick Sale, *Christopher Columbus and the Conquest of Paradise*, Second Edition (London: Tauris Parke Paperbacks, 2006), 47-74; Frederick A. Ober, *Amerigo Vespucci* (New York: Harper and Brothers Publishers, 1907), 237-251, Project Gutenberg, http://www.gutenberg.org/files/19997/19997-h/19997-h.htm#XVI.

[206] GFDL (http://www.gnu.org/copyleft/fdl.html)], via Wikimedia Commons, http://commons.wikimedia.org/wiki/File%3AViajes_de_colon_en.svg.

ward in order to establish an alternate trade route to Asia. He did not attain his goal and died in a battle in the Philippines. After the battle, his expedition continued without him and eventually reached Southeast Asia. Upon returning to Portugal, they became the first to sail around the earth by ship.[207]

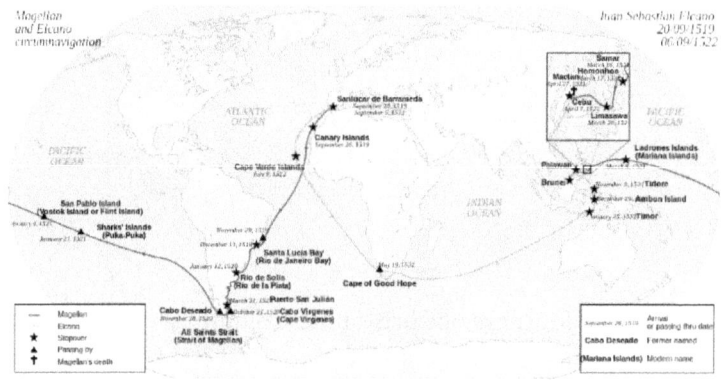

~ Magellan's Around the World Expedition ~[208]

The Italian Zuan Chabotto (c.1450-c.1499), like the previously mentioned explorers, was not sponsored by his home country. Instead, he was commissioned by the English King Henry VII. Consequently, Chabotto is more commonly

---

[207] Nancy Smiler Levinson, *Magellan: And the First Voyage around the World* (New York: Houghton Mifflin Co., 2001), 33-36, 87-96.

[208] GFDL (http://www.gnu.org/copyleft/fdl.html)], via Wikimedia Commons, http://commons.wikimedia.org/wiki/File%3AMagellan_Elcano_Circumnavigation-en.svg,

known by his anglicized name John Cabot. Like Columbus, Cabot tried to find a western passage to Asia. Even though he failed, he did become the first Renaissance European, since the Vikings, to set foot on land now called Canada.[209]

Political Centralization

The medieval decentralized, multi-centric, political arrangement with its overlapping allegiances that often is called feudalism was gradually replaced by a more centralized model, the nation state. The monarch stood at the center of the nation state and was the one who increasingly brought unity to his realm. A factor that greatly promoted this new political arrangement was the long-standing tension between England and France punctuated by multiple wars. A particularly intense expression of their feud is known, somewhat inaccurately, as the Hundred Years War and is typically considered as beginning in 1337 and ending in 1453, the same year Constantinople fell to the Ottomans.[210]

---

[209] Douglas Hunter, *The Race to the New World: Christopher Columbus, John Cabot and a Lost History of Discovery* (New York: Palgrave MacMillan, 2011), 12, 79, 174, 210.

[210] L. J. Andrew Villalon and Donald J. Kagay, *The Hundred Years War: A Wider Focus*, Part 1 (Boston: Brill, 2005), xxv.

The power struggle between these two countries significantly predates this conflict. The French can be considered the instigators of the conflict when in 1066 the French Norman King William the Conqueror invaded England and successfully defeated the English during the 1066 Battle of Hastings.[211] A few centuries later, the English King Henry V defeated the French during the 1415 Battle of Agincourt, one of the many battles of the Hundred Years War.[212] The French, inspired by the patriot St. Joan of Arc (1412-1431), eventually regained control over their lands at the conclusion of the 1453 Battle of Castillon.[213] Their long conflict with the English caused the French people to want a strongman who would ensure that the English, or any other country, would not be capable of seizing control of their land ever again. This wish was fulfilled in King Louis XI (1423-1483), who greatly centralized the French state and in so doing took away power from feudal lords.[214]

---

[211] David D. Douglas, *William the Conqueror* (Berkeley: University of California Press, 1964), 181-211.

[212] Clifford J. Rogers, "Henry V's Military Strategy in 1415," in *The Hundred Years War: A Wider Focus* eds. L.J. Andrew Villalon and Donald J. Kagay (Boston: Brill, 2005), 399-429.

[213] Villalon and Kagay, *The Hundred Years War: A Wider Focus*, Part 1, xliii.

[214] Adrianna Bakos, *Images of Kingship in Early Modern France: Louis XI in Political Thought 1560-1789* (London: Routledge, 1997), 27-60.

Chapter 11: Renaissance

Spain is another example of a European country choosing to centralize power in order to resist the threat posed to it by people who had seized control of their lands. Spain, or more properly Hispania,[215] became a Catholic land when the Visigothic Arian King Riccared I converted to Catholicism and supported the Third Council of Toledo which promulgated Catholicism as Spain's religion. Christian rule ended in 712 when the Islamic Umayyad Caliphate defeated Catholic Spain in the Battle of Guadalete.[216] In 1492, Muslim rule was overthrown by Queen Isabella I (1451-1504) and her husband King Ferdinand II (1452-1516). Isabella and Ferdinand led Catholic Spain in their final battle against the Muslims in the Battle of Granada (1491-1492).[217] Once the Muslims were defeated, Isabella and Ferdinand centralized Spain politically and economically. One concrete example was their enforcement of a common currency.[218]

---

[215] *Hispania* is the Roman name for what is now basically known as Spain.

[216] Clifford J. Rogers, *The Oxford Encyclopedia of Medieval Warfare and Military Technology Volume I* (Oxford: Oxford University Press, 2010), 226.

[217] Clifford J. Rogers, *The Oxford Encyclopedia of Medieval Warfare and Military Technology Volume I*, 215-216.

[218] Nancy Rubin Stuart, *Isabella of Castile: The First Renaissance Queen* (Lincoln: ASJA Press, 1991), 44, 98, 150.

Renaissance Literature and Art

The political rebirth of the Renaissance coincided with a rebirth in literature and art. The Renaissance admiration of ancient classical culture informed this rebirth. A key Italian scholar who inspired Renaissance artists and scholars to love classical times was the Italian, late-medieval scholar Francesco Petrarch (1304-1374). Petrarch had such a profound influence that he was dubbed the "Father of Humanism."[219] Petrarch discovered and introduced to the West several previously unknown classical works, in particular Livy's *History of Rome*, Cicero's letters *Ad Atticum*.[220] When studying the classics, he tried, to the extent this is possible, to transcend the limitations of his age that he said he "disliked" by placing himself "mentally" in the ancient times.[221]

We will end this chapter with three central artists of the Renaissance known as trinity of great Renaissance artists: Leonardo da Vinci, Raphael, and Michelangelo. This presentation will be supplemented by a few other notable artists,

---

[219] Nicholas Mann, "The Origins of Humanism," in *The Cambridge Companion to Renaissance Humanism*, ed Jill Kraye (Cambridge: Cambridge University Press, 1996), 8-9.

[220] Mann, "The Origins of Humanism," in *The Cambridge Companion to Renaissance Humanism*, 8-9, 12.

[221] Petrarch, "Letter to Posterity" in *Selections from the Canzionere and Other Works*, trans. Mark Musa (Oxford: Oxford University Press, 2008), 3.

namely Botticelli, and Bernini.

Leonardo da Vinci (1452-1519) was a painter, anatomist, sculptor architect, map maker, geologist, mathematician, engineer, philosopher, and writer.[222] His detailed works on anatomy greatly aided his painting in a convincing manner.

Leonardo's *Annunciation*[223]

In Leonardo's *Annunciation,* the placement of the hands and arms of the angel Gabriel and Mary are central. Notice Leonardo's use of perspective, manner of contrasting light with darkness, and the symbolic lily in the left hand of Gabriel.

---

[222] Serge Bramly, *Leonardo: The Artist and the Man* (London: Penguin Books Ltd, 1998), 5, 13, 100, 390.

[223] "Annunciation" (1475–1480)—thought to be Da Vinci's earliest complete work.," http://commons.wikimedia.org/wiki/File%3ALeonardo_Da_Vinci_-_Annunciazione.jpeg.

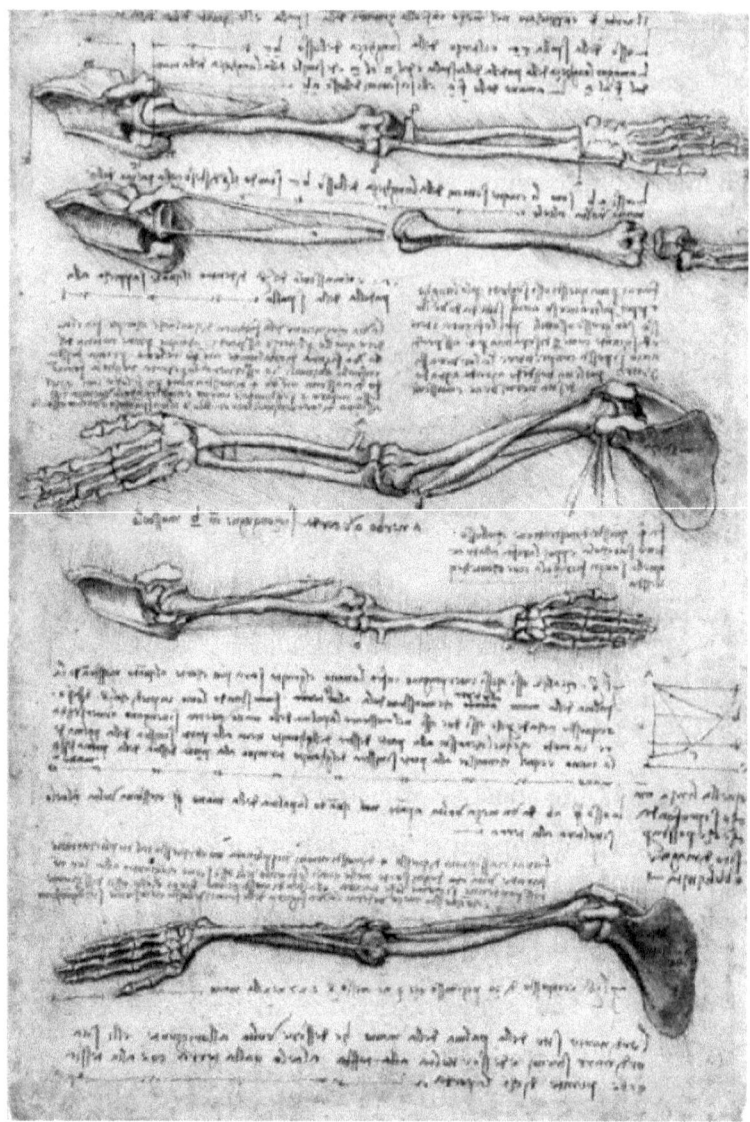

Leonardo's Anatomical Study of the Arm, (c. 1510)[224]

---

[224] "Leonardo's Anatomical Study of the Arm (c. 1510)," https://commons.wikimedia.org/wiki/File:Studies_of_the_Arm_showing_the_Movements_made_by_the_Biceps.jpg

Chapter 11: Renaissance 233

In the following painting are the reactions of the Twelve Apostles due to Jesus predicting that one will betray him? Can you identify the apostles?

Leonardo's *Last Supper*[225]

---

[225] "The Last Supper (1498)—Convent of Sta. Maria delle Grazie, Milan, Italy," http://commons.wikimedia.org/wiki/File%3A%C3%9Altima_Cena_-_Da_Vinci_5.jpg.

In Italy this painting is titled *La Gioconda* and in France *La Joconde*. Both the Italian and French words mean joyous, which is expressed in the painting by the modest smile of the woman. She very likely Lisa Gherardina who was married to Francesco del Giocondo.[226]

Leonardo's *Mona Lisa*[227]

---

[226] William Kloss, *A History of European Art*, (Chantilly: The Teaching Company, 2005), 128-129.

[227] "Mona Lisa or La Gioconda (1503–1505/1507)—Louvre, Paris, France," http://commons.wikimedia.org/wiki/File%3A Mona_Lisa%2C_by_Leonardo_da_Vinci%2C_from_C2RMF _retouch ed.jpg.

Raphael (1483-1520) is the second painter of the Renaissance trinity of great masters. He painted religious scenes as well as scenes inspired by the ancient classics. Below is his famous *The School of Athens*[228] that depicts Aristotle's moderating his teacher's Plato's idealistic views by pointing neither up, like Plato, nor down, but straight ahead.

Below, is a beautiful painting by Raphael called the *Sistine Madonna*.[229] It is currently house in Dresden, Ger-

---

[228] Raphael, http://commons.wikimedia.org/wiki/File%3A Raphael_School_of_Athens.jpg

[229] Google Art Project, "Sistine Madonna (1512)," https://commons.wikimedia.org/wiki/File%3ARAFAEL__Ma donna_Sixtina_(Gem%C3%A4ldegalerie_Alter_Meister%2C_ Dresde%2C_1513-14._%C3%93leo_sobre_lienzo%2C_265_x

many at the Old Masters Gallery. Notice the faces of angels lightly sketched into the background, the slightly interested, pudgy angels on the bottom, and Pope Saint Sixtus and Saint Barbara. To the right of Saint Barbara peeks out a tower, in which, according to legend, she was kept by her pagan father. According to some, the child Jesus has a look of shock on his face, while Mary appears sorrowful and protective. This may be explained by the original placement of the painting in front of a crucifixion scene.[230]

_196_cm).jpg.

[230] Michael Morris, "The Pride of Germany," *Magnificat*, 17, no. 6 (August 2015): i-vi. According to Morris, the Rapunzel fairy tale originated out of the St. Barbara legend.

Chapter 11: Renaissance 237

Michelangelo (1475-1564), [231] the third of the trinity of Renaissance masters, was a prolific painter, sculptor, poet, and architect. He was even responsible for designing St. Peter's Basilica in Rome. Below are three of Michelangelo's best known works: the *Pieta* (in St. Peter's Basilica), the *Last Judgment* (in the Sistine Chapel), the *David* (in Florence), and the ceiling of the Sistine Chapel.[232]

---

[231] Michelangelo Buonarroti, *Pieta*, Wikimedia Commons, http://commons.wikimedia.org/wiki/File%3AMichelangelo's_Piet%C3%A0_Saint_Peter's_Basilica_Vatican_City.jpg; (next page) 2) Michelangelo Buonarroti, *Last Judgment*, http://upload.wikimedia.org/wikipedia/commons/b/be/Michelangelo_Buonarroti_-_Last_Judgment_; 3) Michelangelo Buonarroti, *David* (http://creativecommons.org/licenses/by/3.0)], 4) "The Creation of Adam," http://commons.wikimedia.org/wiki/File%3A Creaci%C3%B3n_de_Ad%C3%A1m.jpg.

[232] Antonio Forcellino, *Michelangelo, A Tormented Life* (Cambridge: Polity Press, 2009), 272.

~ Detail from the Sistine Chapel's Ceiling ~

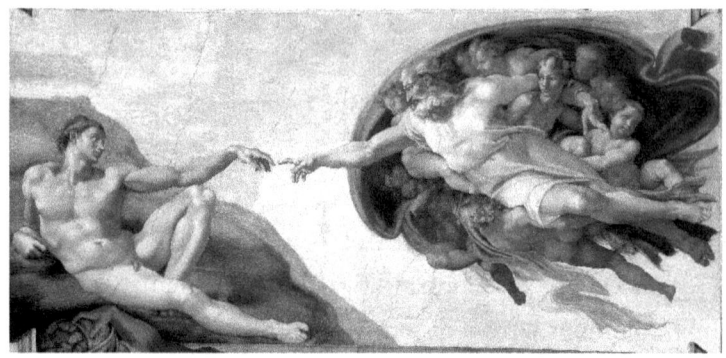

Ceiling of the Sistine Chapel[233] (below)

For an interactive tour, see
https://www.vatican.va/various/cappelle/sistina_vr/

---

[233] "Ceiling of the Sistine Chapel," http://commons.wikimedia.org/wiki/File%3ACAPPELLA_SISTINA_Ceiling.jpg.

Chapter 11: Renaissance   239

The following diagram[234] identifies each of the sections.

---

[234] Sistine Chapel ceiling diagramA1.PNG: TTaylor, "Sistine Chapel, diagram of the scheme of Michelangelo's frescoes. Vectorised and redrawn, superimposed upon bitmap photography. This is a composite of diagram and bitmap images.," diagram, http://commons.wikimedia.org/wiki/File%3ASistine_Chapel_ceiling_diagram_overlay_composite.png.

Chapter 11: Renaissance

J. Sandro Botticelli (1445-1510) was another great Renaissance artist from Florence. He painted many scenes from Greek and Roman myths as well as religiously based art. Below is some of his artwork.

~ *Birth of the Roman Goddess Venus* ~[235]

~ *Primavera* ~[236]

The following painting by Botticelli includes Venus, her three daughters known as the Three Graces, Mercury, the North Wind Zephyr, and Cloris who is changing into the goddess of spring, Flora.

---

[235] Sandro Botticelli, *The Birth of Venus*, Uffizi Gallery, Florence, http://commons.wikimedia.org/wiki/File%3ALa_nascita_di_Venere_(Botticelli).jpg.

[236] Sandro Botticelli, *Primavera*, Florence, Uffizi Gallery, Florence, http://commons.wikimedia.org/wiki/File%3ABotticelli-primavera.jpg.

~ *The Madonna of the Book* ~[237]

Like Michelangelo, Bernini (1598-1680), put his skills at the service of the Church by, among other contributions, designing the Piazza San Pietro[238] in front of St. Peter's Basilica. The colonnades evoke Holy Mother the Church

---

[237] "The Madonna of the Book," https://commons. wikimedia.org/wiki/File%3ASandro_Botticelli_-_The_Virgin_ and_Child_(The_Madonna_of_the_Book)_-_Google_Art_ Project.jpg

[238] Piazza San Pietro, http://commons.wikimedia.org/ wiki/File%3ASt_Peter's_Square%2C_Vatican_City_- _April_2007.jpg.

Chapter 11: Renaissance 243

embracing her children.[239] An example of mythological art is his *Apollo and Daphne* sculpture. Bernini depicts Daphne's desire to escape from the grasping, possessive love of Apollo being fulfilled as she changes into a tree.[240]

---

[239] William Kloss, *A History of European Art* (Chantilly: The Teaching Company, 2005), 199.

[240] *Apollo and Daphne*, Galleria Borghese, Rome, http://commons.wikimedia.org/wiki/File%3AApolloAndDaphne.JPG.

Quiz 11 for Chapter 11

1-4. How and why did the 1453 fall of Constantinople help spark both a re-appreciation of antiquity and a European desire to explore unchartered territory by crossing oceans?

5-12. Choose two European discoverers and write a paragraph each on their explorations. Include specific details from their exploits. The European discoverers you may choose from are Bartolomeu Dias, Vasco de Gama, Christopher Columbus, Ferdinand Magellan, and John Cabot.

5-8.

9-12.

13-16. What form of government replaced the medieval feudal arrangement? How did this new form of government differ from what is typically called feudalism? In answering this question include reference to either England and France or Spain and the Ottoman Empire.

17-19. Name the three Renaissance artists who are referred to as the trinity of great Renaissance artists.

17.

18.

19.

Chapter 12

Fragmentation

Introduction

Unfortunately, the Renaissance was not only a time of tremendous creativity but also one of fragmentation, especially religious and political. A significant form of rupture occurred shortly before the beginning of our chosen date for the 1453 beginning of the Renaissance. This was Papal Schism (1378-1418) in which at first two men, and later three men, all claimed to be the pope. The only claimant who was the legitimate pope was the one from Rome. Although the claimant from Avignon, France, and the claimant of the illegitimate Pisan Council (1409) had considerable backing, even in the Church, they never had a valid claim. Eventually, this issue was resolved but not before creating considerable confusion in the Church and politically, by pitting nations against one another.[241] A main factor why this schism occurred was because of French and Italian rivalry. In the early

---

[241] James Hitchcock, *The History of the Catholic Church: From the Apostolic Age to the Third Millennium* (San Francisco: Ignatius Press, 2012), 216-217.

1300s, the French succeeded in hosting the papacy in their lands at Avignon, even though technically Avignon was considered part of the Papal States. The Avignon Papacy lasted from 1309 to 1377.

Realizing that Rome had been neglected while the papacy was in Avignon, the Renaissance papacy that followed both the Avignon papacy and Papal Schism financed rebuilding and beautifying the city of Rome. These efforts of theirs are commendable. However, other aspects of the Renaissance popes were far from stellar. For this reason, no Renaissance pope has ever been formally considered for canonization. Papal vices of this time included sins against the Sixth Commandment, promoting relatives to high office, and financial mismanagement.[242]

The loss of papal credibility due to Papal Schism coupled with the corruption within the Renaissance papacy was an important factor, in a non-determinative manner, of first religious and then political breaks within the West. (Other factors include the Islamic threat (kept at bay in the 1571 Battle of Lepanto), the invention of the printing press, and the desire of some European nobles to gain control over Church property and power.) In examining this fragmentation that occurred, we will look at Martin Luther, Huldrych

---

[242] Eamon Duffy, *Saints and Sinners: A History of the Pope* (Yale: Yale University Press, 1997), 133.

Zwingli, John Calvin, and King Henry VIII. This will be followed by an overview of the Catholic response to the breakup of Europe at the Lateran Council V, and the Council of Trent.

Martin Luther

Martin Luther (1483-1546) was born to a Catholic family. His father made money by overseeing copper mines and serving as a town councilor in Mansfeld, Germany. From 1497 to 1505, Martin Luther studied at various schools including at the University of Erfurt, where he received an advanced degree in January of 1505. A few months later, in July of 1505, a thunderstorm so terrified him that he cried out to St. Anne that if he is helped, he will dedicate himself to God. (During Luther's time, Catholic German minors were devoted to St. Anne.) That same year, he entered the Augustinian monastery in Erfurt. In 1507, he was ordained to the Catholic priesthood. Only a year later, he began teaching at the University of Wittenberg. In 1512, he successfully attained a doctorate in Sacred Scripture, which allowed him to lecture on Scripture.

In October of 1517, Martin Luther posted his famous 95 theses in which he raised questions concerning the Catholic faith. After continuing to dispute Catholic doctrine, Luther was excommunicated in 1520. He responded by burning the papal bull which contained his excommunication. The following year, 1521, Luther was summoned to the Diet of Worms. At the Diet of Worms, he stood fast to his convictions. In 1522, he translated the New Testament into German and published it.

Partly as a result of Luther's questioning of authority, in 1524, a huge peasant revolt began. Luther responded in 1525 by issuing his *Against the Robbing and Murderous Hordes of Peasants*. That same year, he married Katharina von Bora, a former Cistercian nun and published *De Servo Arbitrio*, which translated into *On the Non-Free* (or bound) *Will*. In 1529, he published two catechisms. Shortly before the Council of Trent (1545-1563), Luther published, in 1543, *Concerning the Jews and their Lies*. In the year of the Council of Trent, Luther published *Against the Papacy in Rome, an Institution of the Devil*. The following year, in 1546, Luther died.[243] In his wake, Christianity and Europe was left divided between Protestant followers of Luther and Catholics.

The resulting fragmentation of Europe and Christianity was not solely due to Martin Luther's efforts. A variety of factors coalesced that caused European society to be ripe for such divisions to occur. The Avignon Papacy, the Papal Schism, the deplorable example of a good number of Renaissance popes had caused the papacy to lose some, but not all, of its ability to be a principle of unity. Due to the

---

[243] Michael A. Mullett, *Martin Luther*, Second Edition (New York: Routledge, 2015), xi-xiv, 39, 44, 56.

recent introduction into Europe by the German Johannes Gutenberg of a metal, movable-type, printing press, messages calling for rebellion could be disseminated with a speed never before possible. Luther and his fellow Protestants availed themselves of this technological advancement more than Catholics did.[244]

~ Martin Luther and his wife Katharina von Bora ~[245]

---

[244] Cameron A. MacKenzie, "Luther and Language: The Printing Press and the Bible," A Presentation at Concordia Theological Seminary, March 24, 2004, http://www.ctsfw.net/media/pdfs/mackenzielutherandlanguage.pdf,

[245] "Martin Luther and his wife Katharina von Bora," http://commons.wikimedia.org/wiki/File%3ALucas_Cranach_d.%C3%84._-_Doppelportr%C3%A4t_Martin_Luther_u._Katharina_Bora_(Hessisches_Landesmuseum).jpg.

Finally, some German princes viewed Martin Luther as a German patriot who could free them from being beholden to the Holy Roman Emperor and Roman Pope.[246] By insisting, in his 1520 *Address to the German Nobility*, that the nobles stop paying fees to Rome, Luther quickly gained political support from German political rulers.[247] For this reason, the Lord Elector Frederick of Saxony and other German nobles lent support to Luther and gave Luther protection at the 1521 Diet of Worms, presided over by the Holy Roman Emperor Charles V. Charles V was convinced that Luther was a heretic. In order to avoid a civil war, he chose not to stop Luther.[248]

Heretical beliefs that Martin Luther and his immediate

---

[246] Thomas F.X. Noble, *The Foundations of Western Civilization*, Lectures 25-48 (Chantilly: The Teaching Company, 2002), 334.

[247] Noble, *The Foundations of Western Civilization*, Lectures 25-48, 335.

[248] Steve Weidenkopf and Dr. Alan Schreck, *Epic A Journey Through Church History* (West Chester: Ascension Press, 2009), 167. According to Weidenkopf, Charles V stated at the Diet, "For it is certain that a single monk must err if he stands against the opinion of all Christendom. Otherwise Christendom itself would have erred for more than a thousand years. From now on I regard him as a notorious heretic…"; Thomas F.X. Noble, *The Foundations of Western Civilization*, Lectures 25-48 (Chantilly: The Teaching Company, 2002), 340.

followers promoted include rejecting the Eucharistic doctrine of transubstantiation in favor of a consubstantiation, arguing that the mass is not a sacrifice, that faith alone justifies, and that every Christian is equally a confessor as anyone else.[249] These and other heresies were enshrined in the Lutheran's 1530 Augsburg Confession.

Huldrych Zwingli and John Calvin

Like Luther, the Swiss Protestant leader Huldrych Zwingli (1484-1531) and the Frenchman John Calvin (1509-1564) were also once practicing Catholics. Zwingli had even been ordained to the priesthood.[250] While Luther was protesting against Catholic rule in his German lands, Zwingli condemned Catholicism in Switzerland. In doing so, he requested that Catholic monasteries be dissolved and the money obtained from them be used to fund poor houses, schools, and orphanages.[251] With respect to Catholicism,

---

[249] "The Augsburg Confession", Christian Classics Ethereal Library, http://www.ccel.org/ccel/schaff/creeds3.iii.ii.html.

[250] Johann Hottinger, *The Life and Times of Ulric Zwingli*, trans. Thomas Porter (Harrisburg: Theo. F. Scheffer, 1856), chapter 1, Project Gutenberg, http://www.gutenberg.org/files/31225/31225-h/31225-h.htm#div1_chap3,

[251] Hottinger, *The Life and Times of Ulric Zwingli*, chapter 3, Project Gutenberg, http://www.gutenberg.org/files/31225/31225-h/31225-h.htm#div1_chap3. "Out of the ordinary

Zwingli's doctrinal teachings were more radical than Luther's. For example, Zwingli maintained that the Eucharist only symbolizes the body of Christ and in no way contains the presence of Christ in a special manner.[252]

John Calvin (1509-1564) replaced Zwingli's leadership role in Swiss lands after Zwingli was killed in a battle.[253] As Luther can be understood as the inspirer of the Protestant Reformation, Calvin can be fairly seen as the organizer of Protestantism. One key way he brought order to the Protestants was with his 1536 *Institutes of the Christian Religion*, which systematically presents key Protestant teaching from a Calvinistic perspective. Calvin's doctrinal teaching is often represented by the simple acronym T.U.L.I.P. The 1619 Calvinist Synod of Dort summarized the teaching contained in the Institutes of the Christian Religion in the five ways represented by the acronym: we are totally depraved, only those God pre-ordains by unconditional election will be saved, by dying only for these elect few Christ's atonement is

---

revenues of the government, aided by the property of the suppressed monasteries, schools were founded, an alms-house, a lazaretto for the plague-stricken, and an orphan- asylum."

[252] Hottinger, *The Life and Times of Ulric Zwingli*, chapter 3, Project Gutenberg, http://www.gutenberg.org/files/31225/31225-h/31225-h.htm#div1_chap3.

[253] Noble, *The Foundations of Western Civilization*, Lectures 25-48, 342.

Chapter 12: Fragmentation 255

limited, grace is irresistible to the elect, and the elect will persist in grace in a deterministic manner.[254] In contrast with Calvinism, Catholicism teaches that, "God predestines no one to go to hell"[255] and that "...salvation is offered to all..."[256]

~ Michael Servetus, a Calvinist ordered to be burned alive for heresy ~[257]

King Henry VIII

Across the English Channel another division, headed by the King, took place shortly after Luther's. At first the

---

[254] Charles Partee, *The Theology of John Calvin* (Louisville: John Knox Press, 2008), 126-127; Noble, *The Foundations of Western Civilization*, Lectures 25-48, 351.

[255] *Catechism of the Catholic Church*, 2nd ed., 1037.

[256] John Paul II, "Redemptoris Missio," no. 10, Vatican, http://www.vatican.va/holy_father/john_paul_ii/encyclicals/documents/hf_jp-ii_enc_07121990_redemptoris-missio_en.html, "Since salvation is offered to all, it must be made concretely available to all."

[257] "Miguel Servet (Villanueva de Sigena 1511- Genevra 1553) Spanish scientist and theologian of the Renaissance," https://commons.wikimedia.org/wiki/File%3AMichael_Servetus.jpg.

English King Henry VIII (1491-1547) resisted Protestantism by defending Catholicism in his *Defense of the Seven Sacraments*, likely written by St. Thomas More.[258] For his efforts, Henry VIII was conferred the title Defender of the Faith in a 1521 papal bull.[259] Unlike Luther, Calvin, and Zwingli, Henry VIII separated from the Catholic Church, and basically took England with him. He broke with the Church not because he disagreed with many points of doctrine, but rather out of his desire to remarry to have a son who would inherit his throne.

When the Pope refused to grant Henry VIII an annulment to Catherine of Aragon, daughter of Spain's King Ferdinand and Queen Isabella, Henry VIII took matters in his own hands by divorcing Catherine of Aragon and by marrying Anne Boleyn.[260] He followed these acts by declaring himself head of the Church of England in his Supremacy Act of 1534.[261] Since both St. Thomas More and St. John Fisher refused to sign the Supremacy Act, they were

---

[258] Preserved Smith and Charles M. Jacobs, *Luther's Correspondence and Other Contemporary Letters*, vol. 2 (Philadelphia: The Lutheran Publication Society, 1918), 33.

[259] Alison Weir, *Henry VIII: The King and His Court* (New York: Random House, 2008), 232.

[260] David Loades, *The Six Wives of Henry VIII* (Gloucestershire: Amberley Publishing Plc, 2009), 45.

[261] Weir, *Henry VIII: The King and His Court*, 347.

Chapter 12: Fragmentation 257

martyred.

Catholics throughout England also suffered in a nationwide persecution headed by Henry VII's chief minister, Thomas Cromwell. Under Cromwell's direction, Catholic culture was targeted by the dissolution of Catholic monasteries and by the removal and destruction of Catholic art.[262]

Cromwell accused Henry VIII's second wife Anne Boleyn of adultery and treason. He then successfully convinced Henry VIII to have her tried and executed. Henry was willing to do so since he was enamored by Jane Seymour and frustrated that like Catherine, who bore him Mary, Anne had not born him a son. She did give birth to a daughter, Elizabeth, who would later become Queen. Without real evidence, Anne Boleyn was declared guilty of adultery, treason, and incest with her brother.[263] On May 19th, 1536, Anne was executed.[264] Henry VIII went on to successively marry four more women: Jane Seymour, who died in childbirth with Edward, Anne of Cleves, from whom he separated because she did not resemble the portrait provided him, Catherine Howard, whom he executed, and finally Catherine Parr, who outlived him.[265]

---

[262] Weir, *Henry VIII: The King and His Court*, 313, 384-385.

[263] Loades, *The Six Wives of Henry VIII*, 289, 309, 312, 316.

[264] Loades, *The Six Wives of Henry VIII*, 289, 309, 312, 316, 335-337.

[265] David Loades, *The Six Wives of Henry VIII* (Gloucester-

~ Henry VIII With His Wife Jane Seymour and Son Edward ~[266]

Lateran Council V and the Council of Trent

Before the Protestant Reformation was fully underway, the Catholic Church had tried to prevent the Church and society from fragmenting. At Lateran Council V (1512-

---

shire: Amberley Publishing Plc, 2009), x-xii.

[266] Campbell, Thomas P. *Henry VIII and the Art of Majesty*, "Jane Seymour (left) became Henry's third wife, pictured right with Henry and the young Prince Edward, c.1545, by an unknown artist. At the time that this was painted, Henry was married to his sixth wife, Catherine Parr," photograph, https://commons.wikimedia.org/wiki/File%3AFamily_of_Henry_VIII_c_1545_detail.jpg

Chapter 12: Fragmentation

1517), an attempt was made to fulfill three goals: political peace, Church reform, and defense of the faith.[267] Reform of the Church entailed eliminating simony, especially "when electing the Roman pontiff,"[268] and by bringing the Church to her "earlier observance of the sacred canons."[269]

The reforms proposed by Lateran Council V were reaffirmed, but in deeper and stronger ways, during the Council of Trent (1545-1563). The Council of Trent confirmed Catholic doctrinal teaching especially regarding issues of concern to Protestants namely, the sacraments, justification, original sin, scripture, and tradition.[270] Penalties for those guilty of grave sin were also explicitly assigned.[271] With respect to concubinage the Council asserted, "In order to meet this great evil with appropriate remedies, the holy council decrees that if, after being admonished on the matter even officially three times by the ordinary, they have not ejected their concubines and disassociated themselves with them, they are to be sentenced to excom-

---

[267] Norman P. Tanner, *Decrees of the Ecumenical Councils*, Vol. I (London: Sheed & Ward, 1990), 593.

[268] Tanner, *Decrees of the Ecumenical Councils*, Vol. I, 600.

[269] Tanner, *Decrees of the Ecumenical Councils*, Vol. I, 614.

[270] Tanner, *Decrees of the Ecumenical Councils*, Vol. II (London: Sheed & Ward, 1990), 657-658.

[271] Tanner, *Decrees of the Ecumenical Councils*, Vol. II, 657-658.

munication and not absolved from it until they obey in deed the admonition given them".²⁷² In the year following the council, its teaching were summarized in the 1564 Tridentine Creed.²⁷³ A few years later, in 1566, Pope Pius V issued the Council of Trent's Roman Catechism.²⁷⁴

Quiz 12 for Chapter 12

1-8. List and describe four significant factors that made Europe ripe for religious and political fragmentation.

    1-2.

    3-4.

    5-6.

---

²⁷² Tanner, *Decrees of the Ecumenical Councils*, Vol. II, 758-759.

²⁷³ For the entire text see the following site. Pius IV, "The Profession of the Tridentine Faith, 1564" Christian Classics Ethereal Library, http://www.ccel.org/ccel/schaff/creeds1.vi.iv.html.

²⁷⁴ Pius V, "Roman Catechism, 1566" Christian Classics Ethereal Library, http://www.ccel.org/ccel/schaff/creeds1.vi.iv.html.

Chapter 12: Fragmentation   261

    7-8.

9. What was the political motivation of German nobles who sided with Martin Luther?

10. What did Huldrych Zwingli propose happen to Catholic monasteries in Swiss lands?

11. How did John Calvin bring order to Protestantism?

12. Why did Henry VIII separate from the Catholic Church? Include in your answer the title Defender of the Faith that was granted to Henry VIII.

13-14. Name the two reforming Catholic councils. The first immediately preceded the Protestant Reformation. The second immediately followed the Protestant Reformation.

13.

14.

Index

Abraham............ 14-7, 24
Aeneas......................... 140
Aeschylus..................... 95
Alaric I 183
Albert the Great. 202, 204
Alexander the Great 31-2, 55, 69, 76, 81, 97, 113
Amerigo Vespucci...... 225
Anne Boleyn.......... 256-57
Antiochus Epiphanes... 32
Aphrodite 85, 92, 134, 150
aqueduct 142, 147
Aquinas........... 46, 171-72, 174, 202
Aristophanes................ 95
Aristotle.............. 76, 96-7, 125, 171-72, 235
Artaxerxes I................... 30
Assyrians 14-5
Athens...... 55-62, 64-5, 69, 71-3, 75, 126, 173, 235
Augsburg Confession. 253
Avignon Papacy. 248, 250

Babylonians......... 14-5, 29
Bartolomeu Dias....... 220, 222-3
Basilica 148-49, 175-76, 210, 237, 242
Battle of Granada....... 229
Battle of Guadalete.... 229
Battle of Hastings...... 228
Benedict XVI............... 136, 187, 189, 203-04
Bonaventure 202
Botticelli.... 85-6, 231, 241
Bronze Age 1, 5-7
Brutus......................... 129
Bubonic Plague 198
Caesar Augustus 122, 129, 160-61, 183
Calvin 249, 253-56
Canaan 15-6, 20-1
Catullus............... 139, 141
Chaos............. 39-40, 82-4
Christopher Columbus.... 220, 224-25, 227

263

Cicero......48, 123-25, 139, 230
Cimabue................213-14
Codex Justinianus......123
comedies......................95
Constantine...........185-86
Constantinople..........198, 219-20, 227
Council of Trent..249-50, 258-59
Cronus...............85-6, 133
Cyrus II..........................29
December..............136-39
Defender of the Faith.256
Defense of the Seven Sacraments...........256
Democritus....................96
Descartes....................220
Deucalion..................87-9
dictation theory............45
Dionysius...............96, 160
Divino Afflante Spiritu..... 46-7
Draco......................57-60
Edict of Cyrus...............29
Edict of Milan...122, 185
Enuma Elish.............38-9

Epic of Gilgamesh........89
Epistle of Mathetes to Diognetus............192
Euripides......................95
Ezra.....................30, 42-3
Ferdinand Magellan.220, 224-25
Feudalism...................227
Frederick I Barbarossa199
Frederick of Saxony...252
Gaia....................83-4, 133
Galilee...161, 164-65, 171
Galileo........................204
Giotto di Bondone....213, 215
Greek city-states......55-7, 69-73, 75-6, 113
Gregory IX..................199
Guilds....198, 200, 205-08
Gutenberg...................251
Hasmonean dynasty....33
Hellen...........................89
Henry the Navigator.221
Henry VIII....249, 255-58
Heraclitus.................96-7
Herod Antipas.......165-66
Herod the Great..........34,

160, 165
Hesiod............ 82-3, 85, 91
Hildegard of Bingen...204
Hippocratic Oath 97
Homer.................. 57, 91, 140
Horace 139, 141
Humani Generis 2
Hundred Years War. 227-28
Iliad............................91, 93
infusion of the soul..........4
Institutes of the Christian Religion 254
Iron Age.................... 1, 5-8
Isabella I................ 224, 229
Israel.........13-30, 159, 162
Jacob............17-20, 24, 162
Jane Seymour 257-58
Jeroboam 27
Jesus 9, 25, 129, 136, 156-67, 170-71, 173, 184, 186, 191-92, 233, 236
Joan of Arc 228
John Cabot 220, 227
John Calvin ...249, 253-54
John Chrysostom.........190
John Fisher 256

John II of Portugal... 220, 222
John Paul II 3
Joseph, son of Isaac 17-20
Joseph, husband of Mary. 161
Joseph Pieper................. 89
Josephus 156-58, 168
Joshua........24-5, 41-2, 159
Judah 17, 27-30, 161
Judges............... 25-6, 41-2
Julius Caesar 129
Justin Martyr............... 205
Justinian..................122-23
Katharina von Bora 250-51
King Ferdinand II....... 229
King Henry V.............. 228
Lateran Council V 249, 258-59
Latium............ 113-15, 140
Leclercq....................... 201
Leonardo da Vinci............ 230-34
Louis XI....................... 228
Marco Polo 221
Martin Luther.........248-52

Mattathias..................... 33
Menander 95
Meno 63-8
Michael Servetus......... 255
Michelangelo..... 231, 237, 242
Mithra 135-37
Montanism.................. 174
Moses 18-24, 159, 168
Nebuchadnezzar........... 29
Nehemiah 30, 42-3
Neolithic 1, 6
Nicholas of Cusa......... 204
Nicholas Oresme 204
Nicolaus Copernicus.. 204
Odoacer 183
Odyssey 91, 93
Ovid 139
Paleolithic........................ 1
Pantheon 147, 185
Papal Schism . 247-48, 250
Paris 91-3
Parmenides................ 96-7
participation theory . 45-6
Peloponnesian War 61-2, 69
Pericles..................... 60-1

Petrarch....................... 230
Pharisees 156, 168-70
Pius V 260
Pius XII 2, 46
Plato.... 57, 96-7, 125, 235
Pliny the Younger 176, 178
Polybius 119, 126, 129
post and lintel............. 142
Prehistory 4
Prometheus 87
Quadrivium........... 200-01
Raphael 230, 235
Ratzinger 166, 170, 184-85
Rehoboam..................... 27
Remus......................... 114
Renaissance 219-43
Riccared I................... 229
Robert Barron 10
Robert Grosseteste..... 203
Roger Bacon 204
Roman law............ 121-24, 174, 192
Roman Republic 126, 129
Romulus..................... 114
Romulus Augustulus. 183
Sadducees...... 156, 169-70

Samaria 27, 29
Samuel 26, 41-2
Sandro Botticelli ... 85, 241
Sappho 94
Sargon II 28
Saul 26-7
Servian constitution ... 116
Servius 116, 118
Sicarri 165
Silk Route 220-21
Socrates ... 62-9, 96-7, 135
Solomon 27, 41, 43-44, 173
Solon 59-60
Sophists 96-7
Sophocles 95
Sparta . 55-6, 61, 69-74, 91
Spengler 9
Stoics 8-9, 123
Suetonius 176-77
T.U.L.I.P. 254
Tacitus 176
Tekton 161, 163
Terah 15
Tertullian 138, 171-2, 174, 205
Tetrarchy 175

Thales 96
The Canterbury Tales 208-09
The Divine Comedy .. 209
The Poem of the Cid . 209
The Song of Roland ... 209
Theogony 82, 84, 91
Thomas Bradwardine 204
Thomas Cromwell 257
Thomas E. Woods 197
Thomas More 256
Tikkun Olam 37
Torah 22, 41, 50-1, 151, 168
Tragedies 95
Triumvirate 129
Trivium 200-01
Trojan War 91, 93, 140
Twelve Tablets 122
Uranus 83-5
Varro 134
Vasco de Gama .. 220, 224
Virgil 81, 124, 139-40
William the Conqueror 228
Xenophon 69
Zealots 164

Zeus...... 33, 83, 87, 89, 92, 134, 150

Zwingli.. 249, 253-54, 256